MW00629161

sandra **martin**

healing hope deferred

Healing Hope Deferred
Second Edition
©Copyright 2005, 2004 by Sandra Martin
Printed in the United States of America

Graphics by Don Day

All rights reserved. No part of this publication may be reproduced, stored in a retrieval system, or transmitted in any form or by any means — electronic, mechanical, photocopying, recording or otherwise — without the prior written permission of the copyright owner.

ISBN 0-9763855-0-3

To the Reader

Please think of this book as a wooden spoon, for the purpose of the material within these pages is not to educate but to stir. To stir a substance is to pass an instrument through it in such a way that the relationship among the molecules and particles of the substance is changed. Let your life in God be the substance. Let the events of your personal history, the current events of your life and your vision for the future be the "molecules and particles" of that substance. It is my hope that the words of this book will become in your heart and mind an instrument that passes through those "molecules and particles" and changes their relationship one to another in such a way as to wake up sleeping hope, breathe life into dead hope and give tensile strength to the cords that bind you together with the promises of God. Think of the book as a wooden spoon.

Because the purpose of this book is not academic in nature, every effort has been made to facilitate ease of reading. Toward that end, sources and references generally are not cited at the point of application but are cited here instead. Use has been made of reference material that is commonly available so that, without great difficulty, the reader may discover for himself the validity of positions and concepts presented in these pages.

Definitions of English words, where given, are taken primarily from *An American Dictionary of the English Language*, Noah Webster, 1828, republished in facsimile edition by the Foundation for American Christian Education, San Francisco, California, copyright 1967. Permission to reprint was granted that Foundation by G&C Merriam Company.

Used in tandem with Webster's 1828 was *Webster's New World Dictionary of the American Language*, College Edition, the World Publishing Company, Cleveland and New York, copyright 1966.

Treatment of the Hebrew and Greek of Scripture has been drawn from study in the following reference volumes: *Strong's Exhaustive Concordance of the Bible*, James Strong, S.T.D. LL.D., Hendrickson Publishers, Peabody, Massachusetts; *Old Testament*

Word Studies, William Wilson, Kregel Publications, Grand Rapids, Michigan, copyright 1978; *Vincent's Word Studies in The New Testament*, Marvin R. Vincent, D.D., Hendrickson Publishers, Peabody, Massachusetts; and the *Hebrew-Greek Key Word Study Bible*, Revised Edition, Spiros Zodhiates, executive editor, AMG Publisher, Chattanooga, Tennessee, 1991.

Quotations of Scripture are from: New King James Version, copyright 1982 by Thomas Nelson Publishers, Inc., used by permission, all rights reserved; The *Hebrew-Greek Key Word Study Bible*, King James Version (see notes in previous paragraph); and *The Holy Bible*, New International Version®, NIV®, copyright 1973, 1978, 1984, by International Bible Society, used by permission of Zondervan Publishing House, Grand Rapids, Michigan.

Distinctions among versions are not made at points of reference, again, to facilitate ease of reading.

Where Scripture has been paraphrased and where dialogue has been created or paraphrased, every effort has been made to remain faithful to the context and intent of the Word.

Table of Contents

"Hope deferred makes the heart sick:
But when the desire comes it is a tree of life...."

"For I will restore health to you
And heal you of your wounds, says the Lord..."

Proverbs 13:12, Jeremiah 30:17

Dedication

For the Lord, Who does not disappoint,
and for those who have loved me.

Sandra

Chapter 1

Hope: The Critical Connection

*"...He who comes to God must believe that He is,
and that He is a rewarder of those who diligently seek Him."*
Hebrews 11:6

*"...Foot bone connected to the ankle bone...
Ankle bone connected to the shin bone...
Now, hear the Word of the Lord...."*

The shock was sudden and complete. There was little room for doubt. The bone was broken...thoroughly broken. And it was *my* bone, or perhaps, my bones...plural.

I laid hands suddenly on the bone or bones in question, all of them in my left ankle, and I said firmly, "Be healed in the name of Jesus."

I waited. Nothing happened.

Again I laid hands on my ankle and gave the order, more forcefully this time: "Be healed in the name of Jesus of Nazareth, the Christ of the living God."

I thought: "There! That should do it!"

Nothing happened. To the natural eye and insofar as immediate and very practical considerations were concerned, the condition of the bone or bones remained the same.

Clearly it was a patch of dry dirt and gravel that had thrown me to the ground, and I was offended in no small way to find myself seated involuntarily in the middle of that patch of landscape.

Immediately before the fall I'd been very near the end of a walking tour of the property that belonged to my home church. I'd just topped the last, long hill behind our church-building-in-the-works. I was moving at a pretty good clip when my left foot struck down on what proved to be very loose and very movable ground. The foot slid away from me to the east, I heard a crunching sound, and I was down.

There were no witnesses; I had been walking alone. Even so, I was embarrassed to find myself, apart from any exercise of my will, sitting when I should have been standing, and so I stood up. Better said, I attempted to stand up. When I did so, the left side of my body dropped out from under me, and there I was, on the ground again.

Bewildered by that turn of events, I wrapped my hands around my left knee and pulled my leg upward and close to my body, to see whether I could identify the problem. To my utter dismay, the elevated foot took a long, weary turn to the left and dangled there, quite limp and at a rather odd angle, not at all the sort of angle at which one would expect one's foot to dangle.

I'd never broken a bone before, but somehow I knew: One or more bones were broken between the lower part of my leg and my foot. The foot was fine; at least it felt fine. The toes were intact. The leg, so far as I could determine, was okay, but some critical connection whose apparent job it was to keep my foot and my leg in proper orientation, one to the other, was missing...was broken. It occurred to me that people who break things in their bodies go into shock, and I wondered, rather casually, how long it might be before I could expect to turn cold and clammy.

With great longing I looked in the direction of a quartet of modular units at the bottom of the hill. There were offices with telephones down there. Before cold-and-clammy should set in, I very much wanted to be in one of those modular units and to know that medical assistance was on the way.

However, since my left leg had little interest in standing up along with the rest of me, it seemed unlikely that I would be able to count on its cooperation during a hike down the hill. Without question, I was in need of help.

In one of those modular units there was a woman, both nurse and counselor. Her presence in either role would have been welcome at that moment, but the units were too far away and she was in the farthest away of the three. She would not hear any call for help from me. Other than the nurse-counselor I was the only person on the property.

To my right was a highway, maybe a quarter of a mile off. The road was clearly visible to me; however, I was quite certain that my presence would be all but undetectable, nothing more than a meaningless dot on the landscape to any driver whizzing by at 70 miles per hour. No responsible motorist would gaze long enough at a meaningless dot on the landscape to recognize it as a woman in distress. Somehow, if help were to be had, I would have to get myself down the hill.

I began to search the area close to me for some kind of walking aid. In the movies, at such a time as this, there is always a heavy stick in the available landscape, some branch of a tree, forked at the top, some crutch-shaped thing, something the hero can lean on as he finds his way out of trouble. No such stick was in sight.

I glanced at my watch: Ten minutes after six o'clock in the evening. In half an hour people would begin to arrive for a prayer meeting scheduled to begin at 7 p.m. If only I could get as far as the parking lot on my own…but, how?

Again I cast a hungry gaze in the direction of the modular units. They seemed so very far away. How long, I wondered, would it take me to crawl the distance? Would I be able to crawl such a long way without doing further damage to my already injured left leg? There were snakes on the property — I knew that — and fire ants. What if I were to encounter one or more of either creature on the way down the hill? I decided it was not productive to think in that direction, so I turned my mind to more profitable activity: I checked my skin to see if it felt cold and clammy yet.

If only I could get up and walk. At that moment I wanted desperately to walk. I'd never before — *ever* — wanted so desperately to walk. My leg was in place and able to do its part. The foot was intact and willing. But the connection between the two had been broken, and without that connection there would be no walking anywhere.

Slowly I rolled myself from a sitting position to sort of a kneeling posture, on my hands and bare knees, my lower left leg raised to make a 45-degree angle with the immediate terrain, my foot dangling and wobbling a few inches above ground. In that position I began to pick my way across dirt and through dry, stiff grass and sticker burrs, murmuring as I went, "Help me, God...Help me, God...Help me, God..."

I'd gone only a few feet when I became aware of a dull ache making itself known in the ragged space between my foot and my leg. I rolled to a sitting position, keeping my injured part elevated, and continued to travel, moving backward this time, on two hands, one foot and my bottom, still murmuring, "Help me, God...Help me, God."

And so it went: hands and knees...hands, one foot, and bottom...hands and knees...hands, one foot, and bottom..."Help me, God...Help me...God"...hands and knees...hands, one foot...

Small Things Not to Be Despised

Anklebones are very small bones, not at all the kind of bones that call attention to themselves. In the normal course of events, when they're affixed in the proper places and functioning in the proper ways, when they're engaged in the business of sustaining the relationship between the foot and the lower leg and allowing the foot to move with the requisite degree of liberty, ankle bones are hardly noticed at all.

On the other hand, when anklebones are not affixed in the proper places and functioning in the proper way anklebones become problematic. In one moment of time, along a path I walked almost daily, my anklebones had become problematic. They were broken, indeed. They were quite gloriously broken. Even so, within a handful of hours the broken parts had been surgically restored to their proper places, fixed in position with steel pins and duly immobilized to allow for healing.

Healing, however, was not to be so simple a matter. The bones were affixed in their proper places, yes. Still, they were not functioning as anklebones ought to function. As a matter of fact, they would not be functioning at all for 12 long weeks, during which time they would be utterly unmoving, sheathed in the contemporary version of plaster of paris. They were down for the count. They were out of the game. On the bench. Sidelined. Period. And even after the 12 weeks had ended, when the protective sheath had been removed, it would be several months before the damaged ankle would behave in anything reminiscent of a proper manner.

In the meantime, my entire body moved at a pace wholly determined by the left ankle. No matter how badly my mind and my heart wanted my legs and my feet to carry me toward a given destination at a given rate of speed, my mind and my heart and my legs and my feet could move geographically only as freely or as quickly as the damaged ankle would allow.

The incident on the hill had been a nearly bloodless coup by which the left ankle had taken the reins of government, this in spite of the fact that the now-ruling ankle was only one small part of the entire walking apparatus, and the only part damaged. The left foot was fine. In and of itself, so far as its own function was concerned, it was perfectly capable of carrying the responsibility of movement. The left leg also was fine. It could have propelled me forward without difficulty. As well, the leg and the foot could have worked nicely together except for a single, critical truth: The left leg and the left foot were no longer effectively connected.

To be effectively connected is to be connected in such a way that a definite or desired result is produced. To be connected effectively is to be connected so that the connection is not merely a connection boasting great potential, but a connection that is active and operative. The ankle was in place, yes, but the ankle was not working. The leg and the foot had been surgically joined, yes, but the connection was a connection in potential only. It was not an operative connection. It was not producing desired results.

Critical Connections

Things that connect other things play a critical role in transforming potential into definite and desired results. Consider this: The body of your car, including its inward parts, has potential to carry you along a forward path. The road on which you drive has potential to afford the necessary resistance to forward motion that makes forward motion possible (has to do with friction and all that). The potential for forward motion found in your car and, as well, in the road on which you're driving are transformed into actual forward motion only when the separate potentials of the objects are connected by wheels and/or tires. The wheels and tires are a critical connection.

Consider: Your steam iron holds water and when it is holding water it has the potential to get hot enough to produce enough steam to iron the wrinkles out of your clothes. The electric current in your house has the potential to make your steam iron hot and steam producing. The potential of the electric current in your house and the potential in your steam iron are transformed into actual heat and steam only when the current and the iron are connected by a plug in the electric outlet and a cord running between the plug and your iron. The plug, the cord and the outlet, together, are a critical connection.

In like manner, my foot has the potential to carry me along any forward path that offers the resistance necessary for forward motion to occur. My leg has the potential, in terms of nerves, muscle and so on, to drive the forward action. However, the potential of my leg to drive forward action and the potential of my foot to do its part in affording the resistance necessary to produce forward motion are transformed into actual forward motion only when the potential in each of them is connected to the potential in the other. That connection happens to be provided by my ankle.

Wheels and/or tires constitute a critical place of connection between car and road. The cord and the plug in the electric outlet become a critical place of connection between the iron and the electric current in your house. The ankle is a critical place of connection between the foot and the leg.

Another and even more critical place of connection is described in Hebrew 11:6. This particular place of connection could be likened to the anklebone in the matter of forward movement in God.

In Hebrews 11:6 we discover that apart from faith — without

faith, the verse states — it is impossible to please God. For our purposes, we will define faith as the definitive and continuing activity of committing our lives and all the details of our lives to God. In Hebrews 11:6 we are instructed that we cannot please God without this faith. Apart from the continuing "faith deed" of giving ourselves — our physical selves and energies; our hearts; our desires; our dreams; our labors; our time; our money; our material resources; our practical considerations; our emotional, spiritual, and mental well-being; all that we have been, all that we are, all that we will be; our plans and our agendas, big and small — apart from this "faith deed" of continually giving ourselves over to the tender care and indisputably right judgment of the living God we cannot possibly, at all, in any way, please Him Who has created us for Himself.

This verse, of course, assumes that we deem it important to please God. After all, He is the One Who created us, the One Who holds all things — *all* things — together by the word of His power (Hebrews 1:3), and He is the One Who sustains life within us (Acts 17:24-25).

In the assumption that we deem it important to please God, the verse tells us why we cannot do so apart from this "given-over-to-Him" thing called faith:

"For (or because) he who comes to God must believe that He is, and that He is a rewarder of those who diligently seek Him."

It is implicit in the words of this verse that there is some kind of mechanism in us that enables us to come to God, to move toward Him, to approach Him. As well, it is implicit in the words of this verse that the kind of faith that pleases God somehow activates that mechanism, which is to say, it sets a man in motion. (The word 'man,' here, is generic in application, intended to include all human beings of either gender and of any age.)

So then, it can be understood by this verse that the kind of faith which pleases God produces motion toward God. At the same time, the word of God makes it clear that motion toward God occurs only if two beliefs are in place:

First, it must be so that the one who moves toward God believes that there is a God to move toward. This is only reasonable. Not exclusively in spiritual matters, but in regard to everyday, natural matters of this world, it is not reasonable to expend energy moving toward something that we don't believe exists. So it must be recognized that someone who moves toward God believes there is a God Who exists.

Second, the one who comes to God, who moves toward God, must believe that the God to whom he comes will in some way reward him for having come, else why would he bother to search out this God. Note please: In the context of this verse there is no value judgment, favorable or unfavorable, placed on the fact that we are motivated to move toward God by expectation of reward. There is only the simple expression of reality: Like it or not, according to the Word of God, the person, any person, who moves toward God does so because he believes, whether he admits to it or not, that God exists and that God rewards those who move toward Him.

A parallel can be drawn between the mechanism of this motion toward God and the mechanism of forward motion in the human body. Let the foot represent that part of the verse that says, "...he that comes to God...." Let's see the foot as the capacity to move toward God, the ability to "walk" in a God-ward direction. The foot will represent for us the spiritual mechanism God has installed in people that enables them to respond positively when He says, "Come" (John 6:44-45, 65).

Let the leg, all of it, upper and lower, represent the part of the verse which tells us that this one who is responding positively to God "must believe that He is." The leg, then, for our purposes, will represent our conviction that there is a God, that God exists, that He's real, real enough to be "come to," real enough to be approached.

Finally, let the ankle represent that part of the verse that says, "...must believe that He is a rewarder of those who diligently seek Him." In this phrase is found that critical connection, that joining place, the "joint," that is, the bones and ligaments that effectively connect our conviction that there is a God Who can be approached with our capacity to approach Him. The connection is the belief, however fragile, that in moving God-ward there is to be found some kind of reward. This critical connection has a name. Its name is 'hope.'

In contemporary history, in common culture and in common language this thing called hope is badly defined and by consequence robbed of its strength. The word 'hope' has become something of a synonym for 'wish,' a "kissin' kin" to vain imagination. The expression of hope has been viewed as little more than an exercise in wishful thinking by dreamers of empty dreams. In common culture, people who hope are the kind of people who buy lottery tickets, play slot machines and do "water witching."

Sadly, rather than correct these images and understandings by moving in strong and vital Biblical hope, the Church has cast its lot with contemporary history, common culture, and common language in stealing from the word 'hope' all the life-giving capacities endowed upon the concept by none other than the living God. It's time for restoration to come to our understanding of hope.

Hope is a power word. It's a power word in eternity. It's a power word in time and space. Hope is a power word that takes faith for its partner. The two concepts, hope and faith, are distinct in operation, but necessarily together in labor.

Like hope, faith frequently is wrongly defined. The error regarding faith generally takes one of two postures. Posture number one: Faith is perceived as a wimp of a word that sees something of how God intends things to be in this earth but stands powerless, wringing its hands in dismay over the gap between what God intends and what is, in experience. Posture number two: Faith is presented as the ruler of all creation, a rod in a human mouth, which puts God at the disposal of humans rather than humans at the disposal of God.

Neither understanding is correct. Faith is not powerless; neither is it God. Have we forgotten the Word of the Lord: "Who is he who speaks and it comes to pass, when the Lord has not commanded it?"

This question is posed in the Book of Lamentations (3:37, incidentally). It is rhetorical, of course. It is expected that the answer will be obvious to the reader: No one can command a thing and have it come to pass if God has not commanded it, or, as the King

James Version of the Bible translates the verse, "...if God has not spoken it first...."

Faith is not God; however, faith is the exclusive instrument through which God brings His eternal purpose, His kingdom and His life into time and space. The power of faith is in its complete confidence that God is God and that no one and nothing else is; that He is the Ruler of all, not One to be contended with successfully; that He is the Absolute Lord, Who is to be obeyed no matter what.

This complete confidence expresses itself in action. Read the whole of Hebrews 11. In this chapter certain men and women of God are honored for their faith. Each of them did something. Each of them did something extreme in obedient response to God. Each of them did something radical because God indicated something radical ought to be done. Each of them in his or her generation effectively represented God in deeds made mighty by the humility of obedience. That, by the way, is a good definition of faith: deeds made mighty by the humility of obedience to God.

This kind of faith is preceded by this thing called hope. Stripped down to its Biblical essentials, hope is confident expectation in regard to the goodness of God. Biblical hope is that state of affairs in which one is entirely confident that in coming to God, in moving toward God, there is reward. In Bible understanding to hope is to believe that God is a rewarder, One who gives recompense. 'Recompense' is something that is given or done in return for something else.

To expect recompense from God is not wrong. To expect recompense not in keeping with the nature and character of God is wrong. More to the point, it is futile.

God gives recompense in keeping with His own nature, character and desire. It is in keeping with God's nature, character and desire that we set our hearts to know Him (Jeremiah 9:24). In truth, this is what eternal life is all about, that we might know Him the only true God, and Jesus Christ Whom He has sent (John 17:3).

It is in keeping with God's nature, character and desire that we long to be partakers of His Divine nature (II Peter 1:3-4).

It is in keeping with God's nature, character and desire that we search for Him. The psalmist tells us that God looks down from heaven, examining the children of men, to see if there are any that understand His ways and seek after Him (Psalm 14:2).

It is in keeping with the nature, character and desire of God that we seek after Him wholeheartedly, with the confident expectation that when we do so we will find Him.

"...You will seek Me and find Me," the Lord says, "when you search for Me with all your heart" (Jeremiah 29:13).

The Lord has not commanded the seed of Jacob — that's us by faith in Jesus, the Seed in which the promise is given — to seek Him without expectation, to seek Him to no avail, to seek Him without purpose (Isaiah 45:19). It is in keeping with the nature, character and desire of God that we seek after Him, knowing and expecting confidently that He will be found.

Here, then, is the reward. Here is the recompense: When we wholeheartedly search after God, we will not be left holding an empty bag. The culmination of our search is the living God Himself. He is the reward. He is our portion; our allotment; our inheritance, not only in the world to come, but now — right now — in the land of the living (Psalm 16:5, Psalm 142:5). We may seek after him clumsily. We may seek after Him with awkwardness. We may seek after Him for the wrong reasons and the wrong things. He will heal us of our clumsiness, give us grace in our awkwardness, purify our motives and adjust our expectations — and we will find Him.

The Lord told Abraham, "I am your shield and your exceedingly great reward" (Genesis 15:1). He, God Himself, is the reward. This is in keeping with His nature and character and desire. The prophet Habakkuk knew this when he said:

"Although the fig tree shall not blossom, neither shall fruit be in the vines; the labor of the olive shall fail, and the fields shall yield no meat; the flock shall be cut off from the fold, and there shall be no herd in the stalls: Yet I will rejoice in the Lord, I will joy in the God of my salvation" (Habakkuk 3:17-18).

This is hope in its essence, the confident expectation that when we search after God with all our hearts, we will not be disappointed. The search will not be meaningless. When we seek God, we will find Him.

The Scriptures tell us that hope can be delayed or put aside. 'Deferred' is the English word used in the King James Version of Proverbs 13:12. Prolonged periods of unrealized expectation can be attributed at least in part to the manner in which believers in the Lord Jesus Christ seek after their God. To wit, we rightly expect Him to appear on the scene in great, sweeping, global, ultimate terms and, as well, in specific, very personal, more immediate terms. We expect Him to appear on our personal specific scene in terms of promises He's given, the fulfillment of His Word to us in some arena of our lives and the movement of His Spirit in the lives of those we love and those for whom we pray.

It is in these personal, specific issues, rather than in sweeping global matters, that we are more apt to taste of disappointment. After all, sweeping global matters are very large and from our perspective quite difficult to manage, so we're not so very surprised when His appearance in response to our global prayers and petitions is delayed.

However, when we're watching for Him to show up in the day-to-day matters of our lives, in the matters that touch our dreams and grip our hearts and mold our futures and the futures of our children, there is the very real possibility — even probability — that we will have to look and watch and wait longer than we may have expected to wait and much longer than we may have thought it possible to wait.

Chronic disappointment finds a breeding ground here. Day after day we look for Him, week after week, month after month, year after year, but we don't see Him. We don't hear Him. We don't understand what He's doing, and because we don't understand what He's doing, our hearts hurt day after day. We become confused or we become afraid. Voices accuse God to us. Some of the voices are internal; some are external.

Circumstances accuse God to us. God's own silence becomes an accuser in our ears. God's non-appearance stands up in our hearts to accuse Him, and all the while in the pit of our stomachs there is a wad of anguish that groans on and on and on: "Where is my God?"

Scriptures tell us that hope can be deferred. Delays and seeming delays will come. Scripture tells us that delayed realization of expectation makes for sick hearts. Again, no judgment is rendered against the heart that has come to such a condition. Scripture simply states the reality — when hope is deferred the heart becomes sick — then we are left to wonder: What are the symptoms of this sickness? What does this ailing heart look like and how does it act? How does the affliction impact the daily business of living life? Can it be that my own heart is sick in this way?

It would seem reasonable that a hope-sick heart can be identified best by understanding what a hope-healthy heart looks like and acts like. What is the condition of the heart when hope is fresh and alive and vibrant and vigorous? What does hope look like when it's healthy and clean and unencumbered by the chronic disappointment of delay? If we can know this then we can recognize by contrast a heart embattled, wearied, tattered, torn and sick from long deferment in some matter of hope. If we know something of what the heart looks like when hope-sickness is absent we shall more quickly recognize the heart in which hope-sickness is present. The immediate task, then, becomes that of identifying the "symptoms" of a vigorous hope, and so we turn our hands to that task.

Chapter 2

Hope at Its Best

May I invite you to join me in a favorite word exercise. It's one I made up myself, though I have little doubt that others thought of it before I did, and that still others, quite without my assistance, will discover it in days and months and years to come.

Because it's a word exercise, it will have a particular appeal for people who enjoy words and the definitions of words for the simple pleasure of the words and definitions themselves. If it should happen that these people love the Word of God in particular, so much the better.

I do not delude myself by calling the exercise either scholarly or exhaustive in its revelatory nature. It is not an exercise by which one can or should build theologies or doctrines or upon which one should initiate religious movements. However, the exercise is fun, frequently challenging, very often enlightening, relatively simple and likely to yield valuable insight into the thoughts of God's heart in a given matter.

For the sake of demonstration, let's suppose we have a special interest in some particular concept, say, counseling, and let's suppose we want to know more about what ought to happen when God is in charge during a counseling process. Should we choose to explore these matters by the word exercise under discussion, we would first get our hands on a Bible, of course, and then on either a *Strong's Exhaustive Concordance* or a *Young's Analytical Concordance*. These are common tools of Bible study, fairly easy to use and can be found "keyed" to more than one Bible translation. (I would recommend using one keyed to the King James Version, not because the King James Version is more technically accurate than any other translation, but because tools of Bible study most commonly are keyed to this one. Therefore, a concordance keyed to KJV is more likely than one in another version to be compatible with other reference books on the ordinary shelf.)

By using a Bible and one of these concordances we would find all the Hebrew words (Old Testament) and all the Greek words (New Testament) that Bible scholars (at least King James Bible scholars) have translated 'counsel,' 'counselor,' etc. Having found these words, we would look at the literal meaning of each one of them to discover the fundamental thought or picture conveyed by each. Some, of course, will convey the same thought or very similar thoughts as one or more of the other words. Others will convey a very specific thought or picture unique to the particular Hebrew or Greek word under consideration.

In regard to the concept chosen for demonstration, that is to say, in regard to counseling, we would find that the Hebrew and Greek words used to communicate this concept:

- Describe a verbal communication involving two or more persons.

- Imply attention to a matter which is not firmly established or "fixed in place" according to the purpose and order of God, with the implication that the matter is being examined in light of the Word of God and in the presence of His Spirit. It would be expected that the matter would become established and "fixed in place" in the purpose and order of God during the process of counseling.

- Speak of intimacy in a conversation. Within the Biblical perspective, intimacy necessarily implies covenant conversation. A covenant conversation is one in which one or more participants are in covenant with God, having, as a direct result of that covenant, the responsibility of integrity toward those with whom they are conversing.

• Assume a transfer of wisdom and prudence from one person to another.

• Assume steerage or direction or "piloting" is included in the process.

• Describe a process by which purpose or intention takes shape through careful reflection and deliberation.

Given these concepts, how might we define Biblical counseling? We could say that God-directed counseling is a covenant conversation in which a matter, issue or circumstance not firmly established in the purpose and order of God is weighed and judged in light of the Word of God and in the presence of His Spirit in order to:

(1) Discover wisdom in relation to the matter;

(2) Use the wisdom to devise a plan by which the matter, issue or circumstance may be brought into the purpose and order of God;

(3) Arrange with participants in the process a continuing communication through which the person or persons responsible for implementing the plan may give account for its progress.

This is what the Wonderful Counselor does when the Wonderful Counselor counsels.

I've done a similar exercise with the word 'hope,' looking not so much for precise definition (as was the purpose in looking at the words used to convey the idea of counseling), but looking instead for a description: What does hope from God look like? What are the "symptoms," if you will, of a heart in which hope is thriving?

In my own KJV concordance I have found in the Old Testament 16 Hebrew words and in the New Testament two Greek words translated 'hope' (or some grammatical variation of that word) as it's used in relationship to God and the things of God. After sifting and sorting through duplication of meanings among the 16 words, I identified eight basic elements that would comprise a Biblical concept of hope. Bible hope, then, looks like this:

Hope Begins in God Himself

(This characteristic of hope is derived from the way in which the Hebrew 'yachal' is used in certain passages of Scripture, including Psalm 119:43, 49 and Psalm 130:5. We included the use of the word found in Isaiah 51:5, where 'yachal' is translated 'trust.')

The root from which Biblical hope draws life and sustenance is found in the heart of God Himself. Biblical hope has its genesis in God. Like faith, it is directional: It comes *from* God *to* us and goes back *to* God *from* us in the cries and petitions of our hearts. Bible hope does not work in the reverse.

God takes the plan of His own heart, puts it in ours and names it 'hope.' We receive that plan and give it back to God in prayer, in obedience, in waiting and in faith that increases and is purified in the waiting, until God gives it to us again as the realization of that hope.

Bible hope, like Bible faith, does not have its origin in us. It does not have its origin in the earth. It does not have its origin in the plans and desires of men and women, however excellent the plans and desires may be. Bible hope is rooted in the eternal heart of God, in His plan and in His purpose, which has been in Him from the beginning. It is good to remember the words of the prophet Jeremiah: "Who can speak and it come to pass when the Lord has not decreed it?" (Lamentations 3:37).

But there is a question. What about the words of Psalm 37:4, "Delight yourself in the Lord and He will give you the desires of your heart"?

Does not God promise to give us the desires that are in our own hearts?

Psalm 37:4 is truth, of course, and there is no discrepancy

between the words of the prophet in Lamentations 3:37 and the words of the psalmist in Psalm 37:4. The Hebrew word translated 'give' in this passage from the Psalms could have been translated, perhaps even better translated, 'assign.' The word 'delight' in the verse is translated from a Hebrew word which speaks of becoming pliable in the hands of God, of being yielded and surrendered to His processes and purposes.

With that in mind, read the verse this way: When you are pliable and surrendered and yielded in God and to God, then God Himself will plant in your heart the desires that are in His heart, and those desires will attract His effective power.

This business of becoming like Jesus — which is the business of all His followers (II Corinthians 3:18) — includes an exchange of desires. Mine are given to Him; His are given to me. As we delight ourselves in the Lord, as we become pliable within His plan, our hearts begin to be shaped and molded by that very plan, and our hearts step into a process of being emptied of their own desires and stuffed full of longings that take their life from God's heart.

When God hears the echo of His own longings in our hearts, He will release His/our desires into the experience of our days with all the pleasure that is His when He gives us the kingdom (Luke 12:32). These kinds of desires we can bring to the Lord and there, in His presence, cry out unabashedly, as did David: "Remember the word unto Thy servant, upon which Thou has caused me to hope" (Psalm 119:49).

Again, Bible hope, like Bible faith, is directional. It begins in God, comes to me, goes back to God, returns to me.

Hope Desires

(This characteristic of hope is seen in the Greek words 'elpizo' and 'elpis.')

Hope is not indifferent toward the desires God assigns to our hearts. "It-might-be-nice-if, but-I-can-do-without," is not a statement birthed in Bible hope. Bible hope is strong desire; it is strong longing to go and dwell in that corner of God's heart into which He has allowed us to look.

Hope is strong desire that defines and gives direction to our passions and energies. Hope wants because God wants, and there is urgency in the wanting, a life-or-death urgency. This is the kind of urgency that sounded out from the mouth of Paul when he said: "I speak the truth in Christ — I am not lying, my conscience confirms it in the Holy Spirit — I have great sorrow and unceasing anguish in my heart. For I could wish that I myself were cursed and cut off from Christ for the sake of my brothers...those of my own race, the people of Israel" (Romans 9:1-3).

Who among us would choose to be cut off from the life of Christ, even if in the choosing we would make a way for someone else to come into the Lord? Such was the urgency of Paul's desire toward the Jews: Willing rather that he himself be separated from God than that the Jews be excluded from the promise of God.

This is the kind of urgency that sounded from the mouth of Scottish reformer John Knox (c. 1505-1572) whose life was forged amidst the fires of persecution and martyrdom, a man who spoke righteousness to powers that wielded bloody swords with unrighteousness. Upon his death, it was said of John Knox that he was one "who never feared the face of man" (*John Knox: Apostle of the Scottish Reformation*, p.124, G. Barnett Smith, rewritten by Dorothy Martin, Moody Press, Chicago, 1982).

This same biography records that Knox had two all-consuming passions: Love for the glory of his God and love for his country. Those passions met in a relentless desire to establish in Scotland "the only true conception of the primitive Church as based on the teaching of Christ and the Apostles" (Smith, p. 12).

Traditionally, it is told of Knox that he could be heard crying out to God in prayer, "Give me Scotland lest I die!"

For Knox the salvation of Scotland was not a take-it-or-leave-it proposition. In the crying out he was sure that he would die of unfulfilled longing unless he saw the kingdom of God established in his homeland.

Hope is not a take-it-or-leave-it-proposition. Hope desires, and it desires with urgency.

Hope is Confident Expectation

(Hebrew 'seber,' 'towcheleth,' 'tiqvah,' Greek 'elpizo,' 'elpis')

Hope is neither a vain wish nor an empty dream. Hope is firm confidence in the Father of hope. It is confident expectation that steers our lives. We allow hope to shape our passions and our energies and even to direct our lives because in hope there is unshakable confidence in the God from Whom hope comes. This God Who has assigned our desires, giving us even His very own, may adjust our understanding of what He has caused us to see; He may more fully define the nature of the hope He has given; He may whack off a corner here and add a room over there; He may expand hope and extend its boundaries – but He will not shame us in our hope.

If in our hope we are bent under a yoke of shame it is because there is something more about that hope that we need to hear from God. Or it's because we have not yet matured in hope. Or it's because we want to see with our eyes before the time has come for us to see it with our eyes. Or it's because others cannot see what we see and we are measuring ourselves by those who do not see rather than by the measure of God, Who gave us our sight (John 5:44). Whatever the reason for the yoke, it is not there because God has put us to shame.

Hope lives in confident expectation and rightly so, because hope, we must remember, has its genesis in the God who "is not a man that He should lie" (Numbers 23:19).

Hope expects with confidence.

Hope is "Given-ness"

(Hebrew 'chacah,' 'tiqvah,' Greek 'elpiz')

This aspect of hope would surely imply that we are wholly given and we are heatedly given, without reservation, to whatever it is God has whispered in our ears. To hope is to give our hearts to or to set our hearts upon some plan of the Father of hope, as a book is set on a desk or, if you will, given to the destiny of the desk. If the desk collapses the book falls with it; so long as the desk stands the book stays where it is, at rest. The destiny of the desk and the destiny of the book become the same.

Hope means we have no plan but the plan God has whispered to us, Plan A. We have no Plan B or C or D — only Plan A. It means we have chosen to believe what God has said in spite of all earthbound evidence to the contrary. It means we will go to our graves believing the hope, not so much because we won't let go of the hope, but because the hope won't let go of us.

To hope is not a tentative attachment to the thing God has given us. To hope is to attach ourselves to that thing as if it were an umbilical cord through which we are drawing nurture.

It's to run into or to flee into this thing with which we have chosen to join ourselves. Even stronger, to hope is to throw ourselves headlong into some endeavor or circumstance just as Jesus threw Himself into this business of being the Word made flesh. Hope is an activity of abandonment and recklessness. It is hurling ourselves off a ledge — not gingerly or cautiously stepping off a ledge, but hurling ourselves off a ledge — with all the violence with which Jesus hurled Himself out of His life in this earth (Matthew 27:45-54).

It's a funny thing about hope: It has a beginning place, and a middle place and an end. In the beginning we take hold of something God has spoken to us; somewhere in the middle that something begins to take hold of us; and in the end we are so woven together with the Word of God to us that it becomes difficult, if not impossible, to tell where one leaves off and the other begins. That weaving together happens in the waiting.

"Wait for the Lord; be strong and take heart and wait for the Lord" (Psalm 27:14).

The word 'wait' in Psalm 27:14 is the Hebrew 'qawah' or 'qavah.' One of the meanings of 'qawah' is to bind something together with something else by twisting them together as if braiding hair. In the waiting, in that middle place between the beginning of hope and its ending, we become braided together with the God of hope and with that which He has put in our hearts.

At some point in that middle place, we are bound to appear to natural eyes — that is, to the eyes in our heads — as unreasonable in our persistence, stubborn and a bit foolish, probably more than a bit foolish, in our expectations. However, "God has chosen the foolish things of the world…" (I Corinthians 1:27).

Also in this middle place of hope we eliminate all options that present themselves except one: The plan of God. As the options pass through our thought processes, as we give them consideration, as opportunities to take those options come along, one by one, we discard them in favor of God's choice for us.

When hope is mature, all options except the purpose of God have fallen away. Alternate routes through life are surrendered. All our eggs are in one basket. That, by the way, is one of the best things that happen between the time when hope is conceived in us and the time when hope is realized in our experience: We get all our eggs together in one basket. We human beings so rarely know what hen all our eggs are under — where our securities are and to what things we look for safety and protection and provision — until God says, "Gather them all up and put them in Me."

When hope is mature decisions become uncomplicated: "This one thing I do…" (Philippians 3:13).

Hope is Safe

(Hebrew 'batach,' 'betach,' 'mibtach,' 'machaceh,' 'machceh')

To hope as the Bible defines hope is to be in a place of safety, a place of refuge. Hope is a shelter. Hope is a place of security. Hope is a place of trust. It is firmness. It is solidity.

How can it be that this place of no options — no Plan B or C or D — how can it be that this matter of hurling ourselves off a ledge is a place of safety, refuge, shelter, trust or firmness of any kind? How can such an activity offer solid ground underfoot?

It is solid ground because it is rooted in God. Because it begins in Him, it is safety, refuge, shelter, security, trust, firmness, solidity.

How can something rooted in God be anything but safe?

Where else but to God could we go and be safe? He has the words of eternal life (John 6:68). What else besides His words to us can be safe, what else can shelter us, what else can provide refuge, what else can be firm and steady always? In whom else or in what else are we to trust? This One Who "did not spare His own Son but gave Him up for us all — how will He not also, along with Him, graciously give us all things?" (Romans 8:32).

Because He has chosen us to be His resting place, He is our Resting Place.

When we embrace the hope which He has planted in our hearts we are safe, however impossible a thing the hope may appear to be.

Hope Waits

(Hebrew ' yachal,' 'savar' or 'shavar' in sense of scrutinizing)

Mature hope waits for the passage of time but it does not wait passively. The words translated 'hope' in the Scriptures are very active words. The time of waiting on the Lord is a time full of digging out and exploring what it is, exactly, that God has set before us.

Good things happen in this time of waiting. We are about the business of discovering more and more thoroughly the heart and mind of God in the matter He has given into our hands. It's a time when the hope that's alive inside of us becomes more precisely and accurately defined. It's a time of searching out, of getting understanding, of finding out precisely what God has said and what He has not said.

May I say that we don't usually hear God fully and completely except in the process of time. May I say, as well, that God's plan is always, without exception, bigger, much bigger, than we imagine it to be. That's because God Himself is bigger, so much bigger, than we can ever imagine Him to be. Gene Edwards, in his book entitled *The Divine Romance*, describes eternity as a very small place in God. Sometimes our hope seems — the operative word here is 'seems' — to have been disappointed because we've

hemmed ourselves in by limitations to which God has not restricted Himself. If your hope seems to have been disappointed just
now, try thinking bigger.

Hope necessitates active, aggressive waiting.

Hope Satisfies

(Hebrew 'kecel' in sense of "fatness")

In and of itself, beyond its fulfillment, before its fulfillment,
apart from its end or the realization of its end, hope satisfies with
the sense of satisfaction that comes with prosperity properly
defined. Properly defined prosperity is the condition in which all
is well no matter the circumstance because God is the acknowl-
edged, more-than-enough provider, an understanding which produces confidence that there is more than enough in every way, in
every arena of life, for every need.

Carrying hope from God is, in and of itself, satisfaction.
Carrying hope-yet-to-be-realized from God makes for a time when
you and God together share an intimate secret. Together you are
planning and preparing for a birth. It is a place of the most exqui-
site intimacy. Bottom line, that's what our life with God is all
about, not heaven or hell, not obtaining and acquiring, it's all
about knowing Him: "This is eternal life, that you know Him, the
only true God, and Jesus Christ Whom He has sent" (John 17:3).

We are impatient in the extended place of intimacy. We want
to see things happen. We want other people to see things happen
in our lives so they will know we're okay with God and God is okay
with us. We want to rush away from the hidden, secret, intimate
places. God doesn't. He is not impatient with hidden, secret, intimate places. They are among His favorite places. He likes to
linger. He so longs for intimacy with you and with me.

Time alone — space and time for our minds and hearts and
spirits to become quiet — time to be still — to listen deeply —
time for God to speak thoroughly. This is what the season of waiting is for. This is what the middle place of hope — that place
where the hope has been implanted but has not yet become visi-

ble to anyone but God and us — this is what the place of waiting is for. It's for knowing Him.

Call it a season. There are different purposes for different seasons, even in the matters of earth. Summer, fall, winter, spring, each has its own purpose, its own design. My dad explained all that to me. My dad was quite a handyman. Almost anything that needed to be done around the house or on the car or on nearly everything else my dad could do. One wonderful spring day — a day that was everything a spring day should be, clean breeze, soft sunshine, the smell of damp soil — he was working on a project outside, in the yard. He was building something, though I don't remember what it was.

"This is the kind of thing you do in the springtime," he told me. "When the sun is warm and the spring is new, you work outside. When the summer comes and the sun is hot and the breeze goes away, you go inside to the air conditioning and you do some kind of household business that requires very little energy. In the fall paint the house, rake the leaves; in the winter stay by the fire and read."

And then he added, "Use the season for what the season is for."

As he spoke those last few words, in my spirit, the Father of lights repeated my dad's words, then added a few of His own.

"Use the season for what the season is for," the Lord said. "You'll never have another one like it. You'll have other good seasons, even great seasons, but you'll never have another season just like this one."

We've said it before: Hope has a beginning, a middle and an end. The middle place is the place of waiting. It's the place where carrying the hope, walking in the hidden, secret "together place" with God is satisfaction in itself. It's the season for knowing Him in the most intimate of ways. Don't rush away from the season. Use it for what it's for.

Hope Bears Fruit

(Hebrew 'chuwl' or 'chiyl,' in the sense of labor pains)

Because hope finds its genesis in God, because hope wants what God wants and wants it urgently, because it confidently expects and anticipates its reward, because it gives itself wholly to the words of God, because it waits and because it finds satisfaction in intimacy with God, hope brings forth.

"Shall I bring to the birth and not cause to bring forth, saith the Lord: shall I cause to bring forth and shut the womb? Saith thy God?" (Isaiah 66:9).

Hope gives birth to the purpose of God.

A baby isn't born looking like Mama expected him — or her — to look. Nor does a flower look like the seed it came from. Nor does hope in its realization look exactly the way we expected it to look, but hope never disappoints. Hope realized is always better-looking than we thought it would be — different than we thought, but better — because God is always better than we expect Him to be.

The Hope-healthy Heart

By looking at this collection of Hebrew and Greek words we can know what to expect from a heart full with strong and vital Biblical hope. Such a heart carries in it a seed that has come out of the heart of God Himself — some word, some words, some vision. It sees something that God sees, wants what God wants, wants it intensely and has a confident expectation and anticipation that the hope will be realized in time and space. It is a heart that is given to that expectation, knowing that it is safe to be so given because the God Who has deposited the hope is not a God Who disappoints. This is a heart that waits and which in the waiting finds its satisfaction in intimacy with the Father of hope. It is a heart that gives birth to the promise of God.

Say to the Weary One...

The saddest thing about us human beings is that we are so human. We are impatient. We are easily distracted. We are easily discouraged. We are creatures who do well with immediate reward but have a difficult time making peace with a reward that seems very far away and very unattainable.

We are sometimes good beginners, but poor finishers — good sprinters, but not good for the long distance run. The reality of our very human human-ness is that we grow weary in the waiting which is necessarily part and parcel of birthing divine hope into time and space. We lose sight of promises. We fail to see the value of endurance. The reality of hope not fulfilled — day after day after day after month after month after year after year — the reality of a finish line that we never can quite get to — these things in our sight look much bigger, much more real to our hearts than the promise with which we began the race. Weariness sets in. We get tired. Our hearts get sick.

What does it mean to have a sick heart? Realize, first of all, that the word 'heart,' as it's used in Proverbs 13:12 ("Hope deferred makes the heart sick..."), speaks of the center or the middle of something. The heart of man, used in this way, does not have reference to the organ that pumps blood, but rather to the totality of the inner man or the totality of the immaterial nature of man. It speaks of his deepest, innermost feelings. Also this word heart is a synonym for the mind or "sense" or perceptive nature and speaks of the seat of the will.

When we speak of a sick heart we're not talking about a surface scratch. We're speaking of a disease that has infected thought patterns, mindsets, emotional patterns and realities, and exercises of choice and of affections. We're talking about communication patterns with humans and, even more critically, with God. We're talking about perceptions of spiritual realities. We're talking about eyes to see the things of God and ears to hear His voice.

From this perspective, my heart is all that is me; your heart is all that is you — all except for our physical bodies, and even our physical bodies are greatly impacted by the condition of the inner man.

What happens when this hard-to-grab-hold-of part of man gets sick? The Hebrew word translated 'sick' in Proverbs 13:12 means literally to become rubbed down, to become worn down, not in a physical sense but in a mental sense. The sickness is an internal wearing down, a wearing down of the soul. To say that my heart is sick is to say that it has been rubbed and rubbed and rubbed so that it wears down and wears out. Picture the eraser of a pencil, used again and again and again, wearing away in pieces, until there is no eraser left with which to erase things.

The Hebrew word translated 'sick' is tied to words that mean 'to bore,' as a dental drill would bore a hole in a tooth. It means to wound. A wound is defined as the breaking of a membrane, usually with damage to underlying tissue. Hearts become bruised in deep places, underlying places, core places. To say that my heart is sick is to say that it has broken into pieces, it has broken apart; it has become divided. The pieces don't fit together anymore. There is disintegration internally. I lose a sense of continuity in my life. I don't see long-term sense to my life, maybe not even short-term sense.

The heart sick with deferment is everything a hope-healthy heart is not. A sick heart has stopped drawing its life — if it draws life at all — from the taproot of vision that is in the heart of God. It has lost sight of the dream, has lost even its capacity to dream. In one season of my life I spent eight years living among children of deferred hope, natural children, young children, into the third generation or so of deferred hope. They had no capacity to dream. They had no capacity to envision life with a different landscape than the barren one in which they'd come to age and in which their parents had grown old. They lived without dreams. A hope-sick heart has lost its capacity to see into the heart of God. It has no dream. It has no vision.

A heart sick with deferment first loses intensity of desire, then loses desire altogether. It wants nothing, expects nothing from God and anticipates nothing.

Because it does not anticipate, it cannot wait. It must have gratification now because there is no expectation for what lies ahead. Having fallen away from the safety of hope, it lives with a continuing sense of impending danger, disaster, grief and/or loss. There is no relief from the ominous sense that something is wrong, very wrong, and, of course, there is something very wrong.

A heart sick with deferment cannot find satisfaction in intimacy with God. If left to languish it will lose not only satisfaction in intimacy with God, but even its capacity to find intimacy with God, let alone derive satisfaction from it.

Thus separated from the Father of hope, the heart sick from deferment becomes barren. It is no longer a vessel through which the longings and desires and passions and vision of the heart of God are birthed in time and space.

In its original sense the English word 'hope' means to leap up in expectation. In the heart sick from delay and disappointment there is no leaping up in anticipation. In South America there is a bird called the macaw, which is trained to the perch. In other words, once trained it stays on the perch apart from mechanical restraints. This is how the training is accomplished: While the bird is young its trainers chain it to the perch by one leg (with very small chains, it could be assumed). When the bird makes its first attempt to fly, it discovers very quickly that flying is not a possibility, so it waits for another moment. Then it tries again. And crashes back to the perch again. And then it waits again and tries again and falls back to the perch again and tries again and falls back to the perch again.

After a painful series of disappointments the bird makes what will be its final attempt to fly. When that attempt fails as did all the others, the bird folds its wings in a certain way, recognizable by the trainer. Once the wings are folded in that way, the trainer knows the bird will never again attempt to fly, so he removes the chains from the legs of the bird. The chains are no longer necessary. The bird has lost its expectation of flight. It will never try again. It would rather never fly again than to be disappointed in yet one more attempt to do so.

Hear the song of the heart sick from delay and disappointment: "I would rather not hope at all than to hope and be disappointed one more time."

He Who Comes to God . . .

"...Must believe that He is, and that He is a rewarder of those who diligently seek Him."

This is hope: To believe that God is real, that He can be "come to" and that when we come to Him there is reward. Hope moves us from the static position of believing that there is a God to a dynamic position of moving toward Him.

The status of our hope and the health of our hearts, where hope is carried, is important not only to us but to God, and so God has made provision for healing the deep-tissue bruising that can come with delay and disappointment. It is our purpose in these pages to examine that provision, to get understanding of God's way in this matter and to lay hold of His provision of healing, for ourselves and for others, so that the vessels through which God's purposes are birthed can be fit and ready at any time for His use.

Chapter 3

Oops! Wrong Diagnosis

"...As (Jesus) sat at meat with them, He took bread, and blessed it, and broke, and gave to them. And their eyes were opened and they knew Him..."
Luke 24:30-31

It was not yet Christmas and already two snowfalls had found their way to East Texas, a most unusual occurrence, indeed. Even apart from the snowfalls, it had been unusually cold that year, and the grass between my mobile home and the place where I regularly parked my car stood up straight, crisp, kind of ever-frozen, noisily resistant to the sudden pressure of my feet as I scurried from house to car in the dark hours of early morning.

On most winter mornings in that year the car was frosted at least, but it was not at all uncommon to find my vehicle under a relatively thin, but wholly opaque sheet of ice. I had a good car then. The defrosting mechanisms worked, and so I would sprint from the house to the car, hurriedly unlock the door on the driver's side, fling myself into the front seat, flip all the heat and defrost levers to "full blast," and then huddle down in the seat, giving the equipment time to do its work.

Because the defrosting mechanisms worked well but not quickly I had a good bit of time in which to meditate before I could drive anywhere. On one of those mornings in particular I meditated upon my surroundings.

The sheet of ice on the windshield limited my field of vision straight forward. In the same way, ice on the side windows limited my field of vision right and left, and as I looked in the rear view mirror I could see only more ice. Visibility was restricted to what was immediately in front of me, immediately to the side of me and immediately behind. It was not an entirely uncomfortable feeling. It made for a small world, only a few feet big, wholly manageable. Once I gave myself to the enclosure of the car, for all practical purposes, nothing existed beyond the sheet of ice on the windows. If my field of vision were to be trusted, the whole world included a steering wheel and a dashboard in front of me, a seat and some doors to the side and in back and that was all. From my frozen-in perspective, there was nothing else to see, nothing else to understand, nothing else that existed.

And then the ice began to melt, slowly at first, so that a little space low on the front windshield began to clear. Through the small half-circle of visibility I could see only a sliver of the hood of the car. As the clear space stretched itself up and out across the windshield I could see that there were trees outside and that there was a tractor parked in a field. Away in the distance I could see a man passing under a street lamp as he walked along a road on the far side of the field, past houses huddled in the still-dark morning.

Wrapped as I was in the quiet seclusion of my car, it was a bit startling to be reminded by the frost-less half-circles appearing on the windshield that there was more to the world than a steering wheel, a couple of seats and a sheet of ice. There were objects all around the car. Those objects had been present in the world all the time I'd been sitting in the driver's seat, waiting for the windows to clear, but I hadn't been able to see them. Because I couldn't see them, it was for me as if they didn't exist. It was a matter of perspective and field of vision. Let's talk about perspective and field of vision.

Definition of Perspective:

(1) The relationship of the proportion of the parts of a whole, regarded from a particular standpoint or point in time.

(2) A proper evaluation with proportional importance given to the component parts.

Definition of Field of Vision:

Simple definition — a piece of cleared land. Field of vision, then, would be the portion of the land that has been cleared so you can see. Picking up that definition to move it from topography to the things of the Spirit of God, field of vision has to do with how far you can see, to what depth you can see, how thoroughly you see.

What Do You See from Where You Stand?

As in other matters, so it is true in regard to the issues of God: perspective and field of vision have to do with standpoint — where are you standing when you look, and what can you see from that place where you are standing?

Perspective and field of vision also have to do with points of time. When you view the matters of God, what is your frame of reference in terms of time? Is your frame of reference bordered by yesterday? Or yesterdays, plural? Is it bordered by your history? Do you compare everything you see today with what you saw yesterday and then interpret the things of today accordingly?

Or perhaps the good things of God from yesterday slip away from your memory so that your perspective and your field of vision are crammed between the ringing of the alarm clock in the morning and the turning out of the light before you go to bed at night.

Twelve men who trailed around with Jesus had that problem. Consider: With five loaves of bread and two fish and some multiplication Jesus feeds 5,000 men. (Most likely the count did not include women and children.) The leftovers filled 12 baskets.

On another occasion, with seven loaves of bread and a few small fish and some multiplication Jesus feeds 4,000 men (again, add women and children), and the leftovers filled seven baskets. Only shortly afterward, Jesus cautions the disciples, "...beware of the leaven of the Pharisees, and the Sadducees" (Matthew 16:6).

The disciples, having forgotten to bring bread for that particular journey, wonder aloud among themselves, "Is there bad bread here? Is He telling us to watch out for the bread because we forgot to bring our own and because the food here will make us sick?"

Jesus, ever full of grace, addresses the concern: "O you of little faith, why do you reason among yourselves because you have brought no bread? Do you not yet understand, or remember the five loaves of the five thousand and how many baskets you took up? Nor the seven loaves of the four thousand and how many large baskets you took up?" (Matthew 16:8-9).

Actually, they didn't remember. At least, they didn't effectively remember. They forgot the five loaves and two fish and 5,000 men plus women and children, all with their bellies full, and 12 baskets of leftovers. It slipped their minds about the seven loaves and the few small fish and the 4,000 men plus women and children, all with their bellies full, and seven baskets of leftovers. Their field of vision was restricted to the warning of the moment: Jesus had warned them to be careful of the bread in the place where they were going, and they had no bread of their own to eat when they got there. It was a corporate case of perspective boxed in by lack of foresight.

It is God's intention that the good words He speaks and the good things He gives and does, day upon day upon day, build in us a capacity to properly evaluate the proportional importance of the component parts of our days. Whether or not the Pharisees and Sadducees had edible bread was not a proportionately significant component of the day given the fact that Jesus could feed thousands of people with only a few loaves and a few fish.

It is God's intention that the good words He speaks and the good things He gives and does, day upon day upon day, clear our field of vision so that we see the circumstances of our lives from His standpoint. From where Jesus stands lack of edible bread in the visible environment is singularly unimportant.

It is God's intention that the good words He speaks and the good things He gives and does, day upon day upon day, cause us to understand aright the relationship of all the parts of this whole thing we call our life in God, so that we see all our points in time from a forever perspective. That's what God intends. Job had a forever perspective when he said, "...I have esteemed the words of (God's) mouth more than my necessary food" (Job 23:12).

Jesus called Himself the living bread that came down from heaven.

"If any man eat of this bread," He said, speaking of Himself, "He shall live forever."

Esteeming or valuing the words of God's mouth, remembering the loaves and the fish of our own lives, and rehearsing the good things of God — this is bread from heaven, and it puts in us a forever perspective.

We forget sometimes to take bread for the journey. Because we've forgotten the bread, our perspective is limited; because we have left the bread behind, our field of vision is restricted to the moment. We don't see very far at all. We don't see deeply. We don't see thoroughly, and our hearts are made sick by a hope we imagine to be deferred when it's not deferred at all.

Hear that, please: When our field of vision is restricted to the moment, to the present, we can't see very far at all. We can't see deeply, we can't see thoroughly, and so our hearts can be made sick by a hope we imagine to be deferred when it's not deferred at all.

'Faux' Hope Deferred

Case in point: Two disciples on the road to Emmaus (literally, 'strong longing,' by the way). They're tired, more tired on the inside than on the outside. They're downcast, maybe even despairing. They had given their hearts, invested their hope in this man Jesus of Nazareth, mighty in deed and word before God and all the people. They had called Him 'prophet'; they had trusted that He was the One for whom all Israel waited, the promised Messiah. But He was gone, dead, delivered up to be laughed at, cruelly mocked, publicly tortured, condemned to the death of the cross, given to the end of a common criminal. How could a man who had come to such an end be the promise they had believed Him to be! And already three days have passed since all of this happened.

As they walk, these two men, they are pouring out their hearts to one another when a stranger comes alongside with a question: "What are you talking about?"

The two disciples are stunned. Does this stranger know nothing? How can He not be aware of the events that have occurred in Jerusalem. All hope is lost. Their world is shattered, and this stranger wants to know, "What are you talking about?"

"Don't you know?!" They reply in astonishment, and then they relate the details to the stranger. They tell Him of the hope, the man, the death.

"And as if that were not enough," they cry, "some of the women went to His tomb this morning and the body is gone! The women said they saw a vision of angels, who said Jesus is alive, but nobody's actually seen Him!"

Now it's the stranger's turn to speak. For a long time He explains the words of Scripture about the Messiah, until, at last, the three men draw near the home in which the two disciples will eat.

"Will you eat with us?" the disciples ask.

The stranger accepts the invitation, and "...as (the stranger) sat at meat with them, He took bread, and blessed it, and broke, and gave to them. And their eyes were opened, and they knew Him..." (Luke 24:30-31).

Jesus! Hope realized...standing right in front of them...walking alongside of them...asking questions...expounding on the Scripture...accepting an invitation to dinner...sitting down at the table. Yet they didn't see...they didn't know...they didn't recognize that everything they had hoped for was, in truth, not dead but alive and present with them and could be touched and enjoyed.

They didn't see it until Hope Himself opened their eyes. And then they remembered: "Our hearts burned within us as He talked with us and opened the Scripture."

The two disciples had left the bread behind. Surely they had heard it, if not from Jesus Himself, then from someone who had heard it from Jesus Himself:

"I must go to Jerusalem. I will suffer many things of the elders, the chief priests, and the scribes. I'll be killed. On the third day, I'll rise again."

It was bread for the journey, more valuable than necessary food.

Blinded by their sorrow, their bewilderment, their disappointment, blinded by loss and having left the bread behind, the two disciples, traveling on the road to Emmaus, were unable to see very far at all, were unable to see deeply, were unable to see thoroughly. They were moving from a mindset of deferred hope, this in spite of the fact that Hope Himself was with them on the road, right next to them, talking with them.

Perspective: The relationship of the parts of a whole, regarded from a particular standpoint or point in time.

Perspective: A proper evaluation with proportional importance given to the component parts.

Field of vision: How far can you see? How deeply? How thoroughly?

Seed Comes Up Different

"...Sown in corruption...raised in incorruption...sown in dishonor...raised in glory...sown in weakness...raised in power... sown a natural body...raised a spiritual body" (I Corinthians 15:42-44).

It is the way of God. Everything we get from God we get in seed form. A seed does not look like the plant that grows up from the seed. God told us it would be so in His economy as well as in our gardens.

"For as the heavens are higher than the earth, so are my ways higher than your ways..." (Isaiah 55:9).

God plants in us a hope. That hope is a seed. We receive that seed and we look it over as best we know how from our own limited perspective — and at its best our perspective, because it's finite, is limited. When God deposits in us a seed we have a pretty good finite idea of what God is after. Then the seed goes into the ground and dies.

Having come to us, the Word of God now tries us, tests us, checks us out, to see whether we are who God says we are (Psalm 105:19). It's in this stage of the process that we can expect to encounter pain and disappointment and confusion and all manner of unpleasantness. It's also the best place in the process to take another long look at that seed God dropped into the soil that is you. It's the best place to look deeply, to look thoroughly. It is the best place from which God can establish your perspective in "forever" and stretch your field of vision so that it touches the edges of His.

In this seed-going-through-death-to-life place, it is necessary that we embrace the work of God in, upon and toward us. Otherwise our finite perspective will remain finite. Our understanding of the seed God has planted will remain limited. We won't see things the way God sees them, and we'll lose ourselves — needlessly so — in pain and disappointment and confusion.

Oh, God will keep His promise, all right — He's just that way — but we won't recognize it when it comes. He'll come alongside us, carrying in His hands this treasure of which He spoke, a perfect and perfectly designed treasure, especially for us; but we will see only a stranger walking along beside us, down a dry and dusty road.

There is opportunity enough on planet Earth to grapple with hope that is deferred in actuality. It's unnecessary and life-stealing to nurse a counterfeit. It is essential that we allow the Lord to establish us in His forever perspective, to look deeply at the words He speaks, to search thoroughly the whispers of promise, so that when God comes on the scene we recognize the treasure in His hands for what it is.

My dad wearied me in telling me over and over again: "Things are not always as they appear to be."

I've found that to be correct.

However, I've found it to be *truth* that God Who promises to appear always does, though His arrival rarely comes in the way we expect it to come. Seeing Jesus when He comes in our midst is very much a matter of perspective and field of vision.

"Through faith we understand that the worlds were framed by the word of God, so that things which are seen were not made of things which do appear..."

Hebrews 11:3

Chapter 4

The Real Thing

To defer: To put off, to postpone to a future time,
to yield to another's judgment,
to submit to another's judgment.

It has been said with the best of intentions by a friend whose heart I trust: "There is no such thing as hope deferred. Jesus is our hope and so hope can't be deferred!"

I understand: Christ in us, the hope of glory…He is our hope …our hope is in Him…He is with us always, even to the end of the age. In view of the New Testament revelation, Emmanuel, God with us, how, indeed, can hope be deferred? How can it be delayed when it is here in Christ Himself?

I understand: In God we live and move and have our being. He is omnipresent. He is everywhere…all at one time. There is no place where God is not, and, from a more personal perspective, for believers in Jesus, He's in us, we're in Him, He's in the Father. How can there be a deferring of hope when He Who is hope is all around us and in us and carries us in Him all the time everywhere.

I understand: Our times are in His hands, and, after all, doesn't He know when we'll be ready for this or that or the other and doesn't He Who lives outside of time plan so well that everything comes together all at just the right moments and doesn't His planning take into account all the stumbling we do, all the backtracking, all the sidetracks we find, all the times we jump the gun, all the aborted efforts and...

I understand.

Nevertheless...

Even as my friend was disallowing the reality of hope deferred, there were words that I carried inside me, words whispered from the heart of God to my heart one nearly-winter afternoon, a very long time before that conversation with my friend occurred.

The moment in which God whispered the words is clear in my memory. I sat facing a window, jotting down notes, random thoughts just as they came. From my place near the window, I could look up from those notes and see, outside, children exploring the ramshackle equipment on a playground covered in shaggy grass. It was a pale, gray day and in the grayness of the day was a sense of quietness and rest that complemented the solitude of my own time away from the responsibility of the season.

The words came suddenly, bringing hope for the future. They were specific, and they were obviously present in the precise place in me where God speaks.

Three weeks later, in a setting more crowded, noisier, God very kindly amplified the thought He had shared and expanded my understanding of His plan. I have carried the words since that time.

When my friend spoke — "There's no such thing as hope deferred" — the words that had come from the heart of God on that gray and quiet day were about four years old, and I ached with longing to see with my natural eyes, in the course of my ordinary days, the exterior experience of the words of God that lived so strongly in my interior. I ached for it.

In this place called time, there is such a thing as hope deferred.

Perhaps we can reconcile the aching in me with the claims of my friend — "There's no such thing as hope deferred" — by speaking a bit casually and not very theologically of Big-H hope and little-h hope. Big-H hope, of course, is Jesus, ever present and ever perfectly enough. Perhaps, then, it would be not excessively irreverent to speak of the very personal promises God gives as little-h hope. These would be the words He speaks regarding the particulars of our histories or of our current and coming experience. Little-h hope would speak of the rewards He holds out before us. Nothing little about these promises; however, it may be that this kind of designation — Big-H hope and little-h hope — can help us come to grips with the gap between the understanding that we walk with God Who can do anything anytime He wants to and the recognition that in this place we call time, created by God and marred by man's sin, in this kind of place delay is real and hearts do get sick.

Big-H hope is there all the time, everywhere present, living outside of time. Deferment is not an eternity word. Little-h hope happens inside time, where heaven and earth come together, sometimes with a great crashing and bashing and not always in perfect synchronization. Deferment is a time-and-space word.

In this place called time, there is such an experience as deferred hope.

It comes, probably, for as many reasons as there are promises of God released. Some of the reasons are common to all men and discoverable in Scripture. Let's look at five of these common-to-all-men reasons.

Corners We Can't See Around

I had just finished laying out details of the vision that occupied all of my waking thoughts. A friend who gives wise counsel had listened carefully, pondered quietly and then said, "If we set off in this direction we're going to encounter some unexpected turns in the road."

"Like what kind of turns?" I asked.

He responded quite logically, "We don't know what kind of turns or where the turns are. That's why they're unexpected — we can't see them."

Hope deferred comes to those who fix their eyes on the part of the road they can see without taking into their reckoning the turns in the road they cannot see and without recognizing that even if they could see the turns they cannot see they wouldn't be able to see around them.

God, however, sees everything. He sees all the turns in the road. He sees everything beyond the turns in the road. When God speaks He takes into His reckoning everything He sees.

Consider Martha and Mary of the Bible, who came to a turn in the road they hadn't anticipated and beyond which they could not see (John 11).

Martha and Mary had a brother, Lazarus. It is obvious in Scripture that the three were closely knit to one another, and why not? They were a brother and two sisters living together, all three of them loving Jesus. Apparently there were no other relatives, at least no other close relatives.

Jesus cared deeply for this little family. He spent time with them in their home and seemed to enjoy the visits. Very probably, whenever He was in Bethany He found His way to the home of Martha, Mary and Lazarus. It's reasonable to conclude that the family would have heard and cherished the words of Jesus. They would have known Him to be a healer, so it's little wonder that when Lazarus fell sick Martha and Mary sent immediate and urgent word to Jesus: "The one whom You love is sick."

The expectation of the two women was implicit in the announcement. They expected Jesus, the healer, to come and heal His friend Lazarus.

And Jesus did come, but He didn't come immediately and when He came, insofar as the hearts of the two sisters were concerned, He came too late.

Having heard the report of Lazarus' illness, Jesus waited two days before beginning the journey to Bethany. Even as He started down the road toward Lazarus' hometown Jesus knew that his friend was already dead. By the time Jesus arrived in Bethany, four days had passed since Lazarus' death. Mary and Martha were heartbroken and in mourning.

It was Martha who first went out to meet Jesus as He approached Bethany. Her words were sad words at best, even accusatory: "Lord, if You had been here my brother would not have died."

To her credit, Martha added something like: "But I haven't lost my faith in You, Lord. Even now, with my brother dead, I know that whatever you ask of God He will give it to you."

Jesus liked the attitude and He made an offer. He offered something even better than healing.

"Your brother shall rise again," He said.

Martha heard the words but missed the power of the offer. She answered religiously, "Oh, I know. I know Lazarus will rise again at the last day."

Jesus baited the hook again.

"I am the resurrection," He said.

Resurrection, He was suggesting, is not a "last-day" thing. It's in Jesus.

"He that believes in me," Jesus continued, "Though he were dead, yet shall he live."

Martha stepped up close to Jesus' words, but not close enough.

"Yes, Lord," she said. "I believe that You are the Christ, the Son of God which should come into the world."

Having said these good words, Martha left the presence of Jesus.

Martha's field of vision went only as far as the corner called 'healing.' She could see that far, but in spite of her faith-filled words — "Whatever You ask God will give" — Martha couldn't see around that corner called 'healing.' She couldn't hear Jesus' invitation to travel with Him to a place called 'resurrection.'

The next words of John 11 give us an interesting picture. Martha goes secretly to call her sister, Mary, saying, "The Teacher has come and is calling for you."

Question: Where does the Word of God say that Jesus had called for Mary?

Jesus had offered Martha the experience of believing resurrection in the here and now. Could it be that Martha, in leaving the presence of Jesus to find her sister, was seeking to escape the pressure of an invitation she didn't quite understand? Could she have been behaving rather like Felix (Acts 24:24-27), who became afraid under the pressure of the Word of God and answered the urgency of its claims with, "Go away for now; when I have a convenient time I'll call for you."

Or did she go to find Mary because in Martha's estimation

Mary was more suited than she to seize the opportunity Jesus offered? Was she then rather like Moses begging off the call of God at the burning bush? It may very well have been true that Mary was more suited by temperament to consider the possibility that a here-and-now resurrection of Lazarus was available for the asking. At that particular moment, however, Mary's hearing was as dull as Martha's.

When Martha told Mary that Jesus was calling for her, the still-grieving sister quickly rose up, came to the Teacher she so loved, threw herself at His feet and repeated the very words Martha had spoken.

"Lord, if You had been here, my brother would not have died."

Jesus was not edified. When Jesus saw Mary weeping, He groaned in the spirit and was troubled and said, "Where have you laid him (Lazarus)?"

As the crowd of mourners, and Jesus, came to the place where Lazarus was entombed, Jesus wept aloud, to the amazement of some, who marveled at his evident love for the dead Lazarus, and to the wonder of others, who said among themselves, "This man who has opened the eyes of the blind, couldn't he have kept Lazarus from dying?"

The command of Jesus spoken at the mouth of the tomb was simple: "Take away the stone."

Martha was appalled! "But Lord, Lazarus stinks by now — He's been dead four days!"

"Did I not tell you," Jesus scolded her, "that if you would believe you would see the glory of God?"

With something more akin to grim obedience than ebullient faith, a few of the people who had gathered at the tomb rolled the stone away from its place.

Jesus lifted His eyes and said, "Father! I know that You hear me always..."

Martha and Mary had rounded the corner.

In the 55th chapter, verses 8-9, of the Book of Isaiah God said it very clearly: "...My thoughts are not your thoughts, nor are your ways My ways...as the heavens are higher than the earth, so are My ways higher than your ways, and My thoughts than your thoughts."

We are not like God. We are not so big, nor so generous. We are not so able, nor so willing. We are not so creative, nor so powerful.

We hear the promise of God. We hear His plan. We share His thoughts and something of the desire of His heart. And then we try to fit it between our ears. We try to measure it by our ability to understand God, which is bordered and shaped not only by the finitude of our imagination but by our human experience, which is limited at best.

Sometimes we come up with a pretty good picture of what it will look like, this dream from God. Sometimes, as God is breathing vision into existence, we actually produce in our imaginations a not-too-shabby concept of what that vision will feel like when it becomes substantive.

"But as it is written: Eye has not seen, nor ear heard, nor have entered into the heart of man the things which God has prepared for those who love Him" (I Corinthians 2:9).

There are corners in this place called time. We cannot see around them. The vision God has spoken, His dream, which has been conceived in us, the hope He has whispered to our hearts is just around one of those corners. It is exactly what God said it would be, and it is nothing like we expect it to be. It is always bigger, more expansive, always more exciting, more dangerous to the natural mind, always riskier, always better, always tastier, always exceedingly, abundantly above all that we could ask or think.

If our eyes are fixed on what we can imagine God's promise to be and we are grieving because what we have imagined is nowhere in sight — if we are looking only as far as the corner of the street on which we have lived thus far and there is nothing of God in view between us and the corner — if we are expecting desire fulfilled to look something like what we have already experienced only stretched out a little bit, but so far God hasn't stretched anything at all, then we may very well be moving in or toward a very real experience of deferred hope.

Hope realized takes longer to come our way than we expect because Jesus is inviting us to a reality that is a whole lot bigger than we could have anticipated.

Our hearts must be trained to look — not for what we can imagine, not for what we can see in the immediate distance ahead of us, not for what we already have, only stretched out some. Our eyes must be trained to the face of God.

"My soul waits for the Lord more than those who watch for the morning — I say, more than those who watch for the morning.... For the vision is yet for an appointed time; but at the end it will speak, and it will not lie. Though it tarries, wait for it; because it will surely come, it will not tarry" (Psalm 130:6, Habakkuk 2:3).

Losing Sight of Tomorrow

The young boy looked out of place in the setting, but He was not out of place. Men much older than He and far more educated listened attentively as this remarkable boy with the child's voice answered question after question. His answers were profound enough; the questions He presented in exchange were even more profound.

This peculiar exchange might have continued for quite some time had it not been for the sudden appearance of the man and the woman who knew the boy, apparently, and who seemed both relieved and exasperated to find Him here in this place. The woman's words to the boy quickly identified her relationship to the young man in their midst.

"Son," she cried out, "Why have You done this to us? Your father and I have looked everywhere for You, and we were sorrowful. We were afraid that You might have been injured or stolen away!"

So they were His parents, this man and this woman, and yet the boy seemed a bit perplexed by their concern.

"Why were You looking for Me?" he replied. "Surely you know that I must be about My Father's business."

Without further discussion the three departed the temple together, leaving the men of the temple to wonder: Who was the youngster? How could it be that one so young could speak to the law of God with such wisdom and understanding, and what did the child mean, "I must be about my Father's business?"

Good-naturedly, the boy followed His parents out of the temple, toward the road back to Nazareth. Although He was only 12 years old, He already knew who He was. Already He knew the end toward which His life was directed. Already He knew the voice of His Father. Already He longed to follow the words in His heart.

Nevertheless, He gave place to the claim of His mother and of Joseph, who, it was supposed, was His father. After all, there was much yet to learn. There was much growing to be done. The season in Nazareth was not yet full. But in time…at the right time…

As He followed his parents out of Jerusalem, it wasn't necessary for the boy to look back over His shoulder to remember the shape of Jerusalem or the smell of its air. Jerusalem was in His heart. It was in His destiny. There would be another day, another visit.

Eighteen years would pass before Jesus, at 30 years of age, would step into the waters of the Jordan River, and then turn His face into the wilderness in preparation.

In the eighteen years He never lost sight of the design of His life. He never lost the urgency of the 12-year-old boy: "Surely you know I must be about My Father's business."

He never allowed Himself to be distracted from the things He saw in His heart. He never forgot Who He was. He never ceased to become in time and space Who He had been from before the foundation of the world.

The road that seemed to lead the 12-year-old boy away from Jerusalem was in truth a straight path to the winding road that took Him, as a 33-year-old man, to a place just outside the city of Jerusalem, to a hill called Golgotha, into the presence of a lady weeping alone in a garden, on to an upper room, to another small mountain outside Jerusalem, and then to the right hand of His Father, Whose words He'd heard in His heart for all of His days.

In the immediacy of day-to-day, in the routine of family, in the workdays alongside the carpenter Joseph, in caring for a widowed mother, in all the mealtimes and sleeping and waking and talking and walking and living, just living life — in all of that day-to-day — Jesus never let go of the things that He saw from heaven.

Sometimes we let go of what we've seen. Ordinarily it's not

our intention to do so. It could be that, lying on our backs in the grass on a crisp autumn night when the sky is black and the stars are all glittery and there is not ordinary sound that comes between us and our God, suddenly we see! Suddenly we know who we are, we know where we've come from, and we know something of where we're going and what God will require of us, and because the dream is so big and the thought so grand, we think surely there can be no price too high...no cost too costly.

Or maybe we've always known. Maybe the dream seems always to have been there, growing up along with us, and so there's no thought that it could ever go away or be lost.

But what we have seen is not for the moment and the moment has to be lived. We go to school. We get jobs. We spend money; we save a little money. We buy groceries because we have to eat. We buy cars because we need transportation. We fix cars because they break. We fall in love and we get married and children come. Promotions on the jobs come, good rewards for good work. Bills come, necessary bills and bills that are not so necessary, but the lifestyle they represent seemed desirable at some moment in time. Demands of the household come and demands of our hearts. And demands of people we love. The days pass so quickly! Before we know it, somehow, we've lost our way to the dream.

Jesus had words in His heart. We have had words in our hearts. Jesus had seen things from heaven. We have seen things from heaven. Jesus didn't let go of the things He'd seen and heard. Sometimes we let go. Sometimes the words that came to our hearts once are still there but can scarcely be heard in the clamor of what some call "life in the real world." Sometimes the things we once saw we can still see if we close our eyes and remember carefully, but the pictures have become buried in the routine. Effort is necessary to call them into view. Then we wonder why, when life is so full and so rich, why is there the deep sense of disappointment.

If we have a deep sense of disappointment, often it is because we have been dis/appointed. We were appointed to a hope, but we let go of it or we threw it away or it was stolen. We were appointed to a vision, but the path we've been on leads in a different direction, maybe not in a bad direction, just not in the right direction. We were appointed to a destiny, but we made decisions and choices without taking into consideration the words of God that came to our hearts for instruction and direction. We thought, perhaps, that somehow the words would come to pass...some way...somewhere. At critical moments, it didn't occur to us that our decisions and choices would play a critical role in the unfolding of the drama.

Vision is a road map. The words God speaks in our hearts, the things we see from heaven — those things are given us so that when decisions must be made we have divine reference points by which they can be rightly made. They're given us so that we can orient ourselves to eternity and to the purposes of eternity. Every decision, every choice must be made in accordance with the words we have heard from God and the things we have seen from heaven, lest we lose sight of the tomorrow that the God of tomorrow has planned for us.

Sometimes hope is deferred, put off, lies way beyond our grasp because we have made decisions and choices that have taken us off course. More often than not, because God is both merciful and determined, it is possible for us to find our way back to the dream. Hear that!

But hear this, as well: It is possible for the demands of the moment, piled up one upon another, to squeeze the vision right out of us.

If there is in us a deep sense of disappointment, it would be good now, before it's too late, to listen. Can we still hear the words of His heart in our own hearts? It would be good to close our eyes and remember carefully. Can we see what we once saw from heaven? If the words and the images can be found, then it would be good now, while there is time, to strengthen the things that remain.

Be Not Deceived — God is Not Mocked

Ai should have been a cinch. Israel took a good look at the city — it was only a little city — and figured they wouldn't even need all the warriors, a couple of thousand would do, maybe three. After the smashing victory at Jericho, how much of a problem could this burg be? And off went the army of Israel…to a sound thrashing, a decisive bashing. At the city gate, Israel turned tail and ran. Did I mention? It was a humiliating defeat.

Joshua, their leader, is found wailing in the presence of God: Why did You bring us over the Jordan? Did You mean to give us over to the Amorites? Was it Your intention to destroy us? Oh, that we had been content to stay over there on the other side of the river! What is there for me to say when Israel turns and runs before the enemy?"

And on and on it went.

God had a crisp answer for the leader of His people: "Get up off your face. Israel has sinned. Check it out. They've stolen and deceived and they have stuff in their possession that is cursed. That's why they couldn't stand before their enemies. That's why they turned tail and ran.

"Set yourselves apart for Me in preparation for tomorrow 'cause you're going to have to get rid of the cursed stuff in the camp."

The message is simple: Sin does not inherit.

Now all sin is everywhere. We know that. And all of us sin. We know that. John the Beloved made that abundantly clear. If we're claiming to have no sin, he told us, then we are self-deceived and void of truth (I John 1:8). This is not a good condition in which to find ourselves.

The issue is not sinless perfection. The issue is this: When God has given us instruction and we've plugged our ears so as not to hear, or we've heard and ignored His instruction, or we've put off a positive response to His instruction, or we've simply refused to heed His instruction, then we can reasonably expect to find ourselves in a condition of deferred hope so far as it concerns the promises of God.

It bears repeating: Sin does not inherit. Every once in a while sin comes up with a cheap substitute for the promise of God, but mostly sin comes up empty-handed, or in a whole lot of trouble or reeking of death.

The cure for ungraspable hope, when it's sin that has kept it beyond our grasp, is repentance. Repentance is a change in the way we think that produces a change in the visible conduct of our lives. Sin means that our minds and/or our hearts in a given matter somehow found their way to a page that God's mind and heart were not on, and so the activity of our lives was not in correspondence with God's nature and character. Repentance means that our minds and hearts in that matter have found the way back to the page God's mind and heart are on. As a result, the visible conduct of our lives comes into correspondence with the nature and character of God.

It's this simple: We're on a collision course with hope that the God of hope has set before us. Sin takes us off course. Repentance puts us back on course. When sin has captured our energy and attention it is good to "Remember therefore from where (we) have fallen; and repent and do the first works..." (Revelation 2:5a).

Belief is as Belief Does

I remember it so clearly. I was sitting in a car in the parking lot of a grocery store. My friend, who was driving, was making a quick run for a sack-full of groceries. I don't like grocery stores and I didn't have to go to the grocery store that day, so I waited in the car for my friend to return.

I remember that those particular days of my life were pretty scary days, pretty turbulent days, and I remember that I spent a great deal of energy fending off the churning that was going on in my gut. That being the case, it seemed good, while I was waiting for my friend, to spend a little time in my Bible.

I don't remember in what book, chapter and verse I was reading at that particular moment, nor do I remember whether the text had anything at all to do with belief and unbelief. I do remember vividly that there swept over me, without natural cause, a massive sense of myself as a disastrously unbelieving person. It came in on a wave of fear and despair, and I cried aloud, "OH, GOD! I AM SO FULL OF UNBELIEF!"

The sound of my own voice propelled me to greater sorrow. Still alone in the car, I began to sob. Hot tears ran down my face and I cried out again and again, "OH, GOD! I AM SO FULL OF UNBELIEF! I AM SO FULL OF UNBELIEF!"

Then, very quietly, these words came to my spirit.

"No, you're not."

The flow of tears stopped abruptly. The intensity of the moment went away as quickly as it had come.

"I'm not?" I asked.

The words came again, this time followed by an explanation.

"No, you're not. If you were full of unbelief you would not be doing the things you're doing."

I reviewed: What was I doing? I was living in the midst of some very unlovable people, serving them in the practical insufficiency of their everyday lives, cleaning houses, running errands, reading papers and letters for them when their reading skills fell short. I was serving them in the Word of God, teaching, counseling, mourning with them in right and appropriate ways, at right and appropriate times. I was rejoicing with them as they came, one by one, to recognize the hand of God in the activity of their days. I had given myself to a people, to a community, and God had raised up an expression of New Testament life. It was a bit ragged in places, yes; it was scruffy sometimes, yes, and chaotic. Nevertheless, it was an expression of New Testament life.

As I thought on these things, the understanding came — not new to me, but fresh: Belief and unbelief are not related to the currents that churn and swirl in our stomachs — that is to say, in our emotions — or in our minds, in our thoughts.

Belief and unbelief have to do with obedience and disobedience. Belief, faith, hears the words of God and does what God says to do. It does things which, by God's indication, lead to the goal He has set before us. Unbelief may hear the words of God and may see the goal, but unbelief doesn't do. It fails to take action, or fails to take appropriate action.

"Show me your faith without your works and I will show you my faith by my works," the author of the Book of James writes.

Hebrews 11 often is described as "the roll call of faith." Read the chapter slowly. Everyone on the roster does something. By faith Abel offered sacrifice...by faith Noah prepared an ark...by faith Abraham went out of his country when he was called to go out and sojourned by faith in the land of promise, as in a strange country...by faith Sarah received strength to conceive...by faith Isaac blessed his sons...by faith Jacob worshiped...by faith Joseph gave instructions concerning his bones, that they should be buried in the land of his fathers...by faith Moses was hidden and then placed in a basket in a river, his life being thus preserved...by faith Rahab received the spies with peace.

Belief acts. It does things according to the Word and the words of God.

Mark 11:23, the words of Jesus: "For assuredly, I say to you, whoever says to this mountain, 'Be removed and be cast into the sea,' and does not doubt in his heart, but believes that those things he says will come to pass, he will have whatever he says."

My pastor tells me the Greek word for 'doubt,' 'diakrino,' involves three activities — hesitation, evaluation and separation. This is the path by which 'diakrino,' doubt, becomes 'apistia,' unbelief.

Consider, in this regard, the children of Israel camped for the first time at the threshold of the promise of God (Numbers 13-14). This is the consummate hope-deferred congregation. For 400 years the nation had waited to experience the fulfillment of God's promise to take them out of slavery in Egypt and into the land He said He would give them (Genesis 15:13-16). He promised not only to bring them out from under the hand of their taskmasters, but to bring them out wealthy. In that 400-year gap between promise and experience, the bondage suffered by the children of Israel became increasingly unreasonable and the oppression increasingly cruel. At last, however, God did what He said He would do and Israel walked out of Egypt, free.

Once out of Egypt, however, the people of the God of Abraham didn't like anything about the plan of the God of Abraham. They didn't like the scenery that was part of the plan. They didn't like the food that came with the plan. They didn't like the rules that gave order to the plan. They didn't like the leadership that administered the plan, and when they finally got a good look at the land itself, they didn't like that either. The walls around the cities were too high, the people were too strong, the giants were too giant.

The consensus was unmistakably clear: Yes, but...

"Yes, God said this is our land, but we are not able to take it."

Doubt, 'diakrino,' takes just a moment to survey God's plan in light of human resources available. It hesitates. But God doesn't expect us to execute His plan with human resources. He gives us the plan so we can cooperate with Him as He brings His limitless resources to bear in the execution of that plan. Doubt looks at itself, looks at the plan and reasonably concludes, "We can't do it." It evaluates.

Having hesitated long enough to take a look at the plan in the light of its own resources and having evaluated the plan as not possible, doubt then separates itself from the plan of God. It has now become 'apistia,' unbelief.

There's more.

Unbelief goes on to slander the promise of God with this kind of message: It wasn't a good promise, anyway. The children of Israel put it this way: "The land eats up the people who live in it."

Having slandered the promise of God, unbelief then slanders the God of the promise: "Why did God bring us to this land to be killed?" He is an unkind, even a murderous God, says unbelief, and it comes up with a plan of its own.

"Let's go back to where we were before. We were better off there."

Unbelief does not inherit. Unbelief stands at the border of God's promise, looks in and turns back. God holds out a hand filled with hope. Belief takes action according to the hope. Unbelief takes action also — in opposition to the hope. To move in opposition to something is to move contrary to the interest and design of the someone who's orchestrating the something.

It bears repeating: Unbelief does not inherit.

God's remedy for unbelief is a wilderness that kills everything contrary in interest and design to the hope He offers. The children of Israel lost an entire generation to that kind of wilderness. What will we lose?

Think 'Us' – God Does!

Jesus is the greatest realist that has ever lived. He looks reality square in the face, calls it what it is, nothing more and nothing less, and then deals with it from the perspective of the throne of God.

We're to be just like Him. One of the realities we must look in the face is this one: The theme of my walk with God is not, in the words of a song from the 70's, "Me and Jesus got our own thing going." Rather, the theme of our walk with God is, "...that they all may be one as You, Father, are in Me and I in You, that they also may be one in Us..." (John 17:21).

God is a corporate thinker.

Corporate: Latin, 'corporatus,' from 'corporor,' to be shaped into a body (Webster's 1828).

Corporate: United in a body, or community, as a number of individuals who are empowered to transact business as an individual (Webster's 1828).

Listen to the theme song of the body of Christ:

"...We, being many, are one body in Christ, and individually members one of another....God has set the members, each one of them, in the body just as He desired. There are many members, yet one body....the Church, which is His body, the fullness of Him who fills all in all."

"...(Jesus) is the Head...from whom the whole body, joined and knit together by what every joint supplies, according to the effective working by which every part does its share, causes growth of the body for the edifying of itself in love" (Romans 12:5; I Corinthians 12:18, 20; Ephesians 1:22-23; Ephesians 4:15-16).

God is a corporate thinker.

Isaiah 6:8a: "Also I heard the voice of the Lord, saying: 'Whom shall I send, and who will go for Us?'"

We are made in God's image. Think of it: Your eyes look at a travel map and see England, maybe London. That big, black blot called London registers in your brain and your brain thinks, "That would be a good place to go!" Your eyes and your brain are already packed and on their way to the airport, but your eyes and your brain aren't going anywhere unless your hands and your feet and your heart and your kidneys and your back all go there, too.

We are designed to be corporate thinkers. The individual is important to God, yes. Your individual vision and mine are important to God, most certainly. That you and I as individuals experience the presence, promises and anointing of God is important to Him, of course.

However, God has set me into the body of Christ in the earth as it has pleased Him. My vision and my personal experience of His presence, promises and anointing are part of a larger picture. My experience in God and your experience in God are interrelated. They cannot be untangled one from the other — not successfully, not profitably, not fruitfully. My personal hope, given me in Jesus, is interrelated with your personal hope, given you in Jesus, and your hope and my hope — our hope — is interrelated with the corporate hope of whatever local portion of the universal 'corporate' into which God has placed us, as well as with the hope of the universal 'corporate.' We are members one of another. The eyes, the brain, the heart, hands, feet, liver, kidneys, back, toes, kneecaps, tendons, ligaments, bones — they all move together.

Sometimes delay, deferment, postponement comes because I'm being fitted together with you and you with me. In fact, I would dare say that most delay and postponement comes because God is about the business of aligning us together in proper fashion.

"...The whole body, joined and knit together by what every joint supplies, according to the effective working by which every part does its share, causes growth of the body for the edifying of itself in love" (Ephesians 4:16).

Consider Joshua and Caleb. You know the story. It's found in Numbers 13-14. Israel has come to the threshold of promise. She stands at the border of a land about which God has said, "I'm giving it to you — go in and possess it."

Joshua and Caleb and 10 other leaders among the people, one from each of the 12 tribes of Israel, are assigned to go survey the scene, to find out what the land is like. They're to come back with a report: Are the people who live there strong or weak, few or many? Is the land rich or poor? Are there forests there or not?

And they are told: Be of good courage and bring back some of the fruit of the land.

All 12 of these "spies" set their feet down in the same land at the same time. All 12 of them walked around and looked around in the promise of God. Together they brought back grapes so big that one bunch had to be carried on a pole between two men.

Twelve men — same experience — two different reports.

Ten spies saw a people much stronger than the people of God. Joshua and Caleb saw God.

Ten spies saw great walled cities. Joshua and Caleb saw God.

Ten spies saw giants. Joshua and Caleb saw God.

Ten spies saw a land that would eat them up. Joshua and Caleb saw God. Ten spies saw themselves as grasshoppers in comparison with the people of the land and the giants. Joshua and Caleb saw Israel as rightful owners of the land by the decree of God for whom nothing is too hard.

Ten spies were convinced: God brought us here to kill us.

Joshua and Caleb were convinced: God promised us the land. Let's go get it.

Joshua and Caleb alone of that generation carried the unshakable confidence that God would do exactly as He had said He would do. Joshua and Caleb alone of that generation were ready to receive the hope that God had set before them. Joshua and Caleb alone of that generation would inherit the promise of God.

But first...

God would bring judgment to bear on the unbelief of a nation. That generation of Israel of which Joshua and Caleb were part, along with their children and grandchildren, would walk 40 years in the wilderness, outside the promise of God. Joshua and Caleb alone in their generation were ready to receive the hope of God and walk in it; nevertheless, Joshua and Caleb, right along with an entire generation of unbelief, would take every step of that 40-year walk.

During those 40 years, they would see the blessing of God upon obedience and the unmistakable verdict of the Lord handed down to disobedience. They would see babies born. They would see people die. They would see children grow to maturity. They would see more people die. It has been calculated that more than

3,000 people everyday fell dead in the wilderness or were swallowed up by the earth or otherwise destroyed. The two men who believed God would walk every step through the wilderness with the men and women of Israel that didn't believe God.

My pastor is consistently fond of saying near the end of a Sunday morning service: God will hold up a whole group of people just to bless one man or one woman. By the record we know that God also will hold up two men as He waits for a believing generation to be raised up.

Why was it necessary for Joshua and Caleb, who were of a "different spirit" than the others, to endure the same long wilderness journey?

The answer: The anointing to possess the land of God's promise was on a people. It was on a nation, not on two individuals. Joshua and Caleb were ready to inherit; the nation wasn't. Along with the nation of which they were "members one of another," Joshua and Caleb walked and waited.

Pregnant women and the people who love them will understand. The mother's mind is ready for that baby to be delivered long before her womb is ready. The mind waits on the womb. Her first-grader is ready to start school long before Mom is ready to let go. Both of them, together, wait on the due season.

In the body of Christ in the earth we go together into the promise of God. Some are ready earlier than others. Some think they're ready before they are. Some are ready but they think they're not. Some are not ready and some don't want to be ready. We go together. Some wait. Some hurry to catch up. Together we go in. It's because we go together that our examination of the healing of hope deferred finds its platform in Israel's corporate experience as recorded in the last chapters of Deuteronomy and the first five chapters of Joshua, as Israel ends the wilderness time and begins to possess the land.

Make note of this: Should we come to the border of the promise of God only to turn back in unbelief, we've turned ourselves toward a wilderness.

We've mentioned it before, this killing wilderness. Things die here. Everything that prevents us from entering in and walking around in and exercising dominion in the promise of God falls dead in this wilderness. Every unbelieving thought, every unbelieving bone, every unbelieving complaint, every unbelieving whine, every nagging question as to the goodness of God's motive toward us, every plan that we think might work better than God's, every accusation regarding God's character and nature, every slander directed against His goodness and His power, every sliver of wavering, every ounce of distractibility, every throne that challenges God's — all of it falls dead.

In this same wilderness where things die, things also are born. Something is generated. A "generation" occurs. There is generated a voice that says with confidence, "That promise belongs to me. The hope is mine and it's to be possessed. Give me that mountain. In Christ I can take it. In Christ I can keep it."

In the wilderness things are born and come to maturity — things that inherit — things like faith with humility, readiness to obey, understanding of God's nature and character and ways, yearning for the promise of God that dwarfs whatever difficulty we find along the way to the promise.

Things die in the wilderness; things are born in the wilderness. When the wilderness is done with its work, we come again to the borders of our hope. Only this time, we come with "a different spirit," for it is God who has worked in us and on us, filling us not only with the will but with the ability to do what He has given us to do (Philippians 2:13).

"...Therefore will the Lord wait, that He may be gracious unto you..." (Isaiah 30:18).

It is in this place that we find the children of Israel in the last pages of the Book of Deuteronomy. The wilderness has done its work. All that had to die there is dead; that which had to be born there has been born. The Lord having waited, Israel has come again to the border of her land, this time with a different spirit.

Chapter 5

The Bone-jarring God

"So Moses the servant of the Lord died there in the land of Moab...
And (the Lord) buried him in a valley in the land
of Moab...
And the children of Israel wept for Moses in the plains of Moab thirty
days. So the days of weeping and mourning for Moses ended."

"After the death of Moses...the Lord spoke to Joshua...saying, Moses
my servant is dead. Now therefore, arise, go over this Jordan..."
(Deuteronomy 34:5-6,8, Joshua 1:1-2)

I have this jar of peanut butter. It's a brand new jar of peanut
butter, the best kind. Four times I've taken it out of the cupboard.
Four times I've tried to open it. It's stuck. Really stuck!

I've tried opening it with my bare hands, by brute force. That
didn't work. I've tried running hot water over the lid so something
or other would shrink — whatever it is that's supposed to shrink
— or get slippery — or whatever it's supposed to do when you run
hot water over the lid to get the jar open. That didn't work either.
I tried using one of those rubber grips, specially designed to open
jars that are stuck. I tried two of them. It didn't work.

I've been as gentle with the jar of peanut butter as I can be. I'm
going to whack it today. I'm not mad. I don't want to hurt the jar.
But what's inside is good, and I want to get at it and I can't get
at it, 'cause the lid of the jar is stuck. Whacking will work when
nothing else will.

Let the Healing Begin

I wonder: When the children of Israel arrived the second time at the edge of Canaan, were they really ready to look over across the Jordan, into the promise of God? Were they ready to view the land with high expectation?

I wonder: What was the condition of the corporate heart as the nation stood together in the plains of Moab?

Think of it. And remember, this is the ultimate hope-deferred generation — 400 years in slavery and oppression:

- When, suddenly, the promise of deliverance was laid at their feet by this man Moses...

- The promise was theirs for the taking and they took it...

- Only to find themselves delayed by Pharoah of the hardened heart...

- Delayed through 10 plagues, which were not their doing and about which they were not consulted...

- A hurried departure from a land that had been home. However bad a home it had been, it had been home for 400 years...

- Ah, but a wealthy departure, with the riches of Egypt, just as God had said to Abraham hundreds of years before. Things were looking up for Israel!...

- The heady stuff of escape! Only to be hunted down by the familiar oppressor...

- Another escape, this time with all the drama of the Red Sea rushing and climbing to high walls on their right and on their left, leaving dry ground for their feet...

- A trek through the wilderness to look around in and to taste the promise of God...

- Only to be turned back to the wilderness by their own unbelief...

- Forty years of walking and waiting and warring and experiencing the covenant of God, both the blessing of obedience and the curse of disobedience...

- Forty years of death...

- Forty years of the relentless daily-ness of life...

- Forty years of camp and move...camp and move...camp and move...

- Now here they are again, at the edge of Canaan! The promise is there, right over there, right across the river!

So Moses gets them ready. He reviews their history with God. He reinforces the covenant with the One who has brought them to this place and then Moses tells the people, "God has said I can't go into the land. Joshua will take it from here" (Deuteronomy 31:1-3).

Joshua receives a charge both from Moses and God Himself (Deuteronomy 31:7, 14, 23); Moses releases a song, blesses the people and goes off to Mount Nebo, to die (Deuteronomy 32-34).

And for 30 days the people weep for Moses. Here is a people whose entire history is one of postponement. They were born — many of them — they have come to maturity or they've gone to wilderness graves in a corporate state of delay.

"Yes, there's the hope! Yes, we saw it! Yes, we tasted it! We can't go back; God won't let us — but we've been unable to go forward to seize that which has been promised."

This is the cry from a wilderness of hope deferred. The border behind is the place where first we could see something of what God had set before us. Once we have glimpsed something of the purpose of God we can never go back to the place where we have not seen, where we have not known. The border behind us is what we have seen of God's heart. The border in front is the hope itself, beyond our reach.

Israel had lived 40 corporate years in this kind of wilderness. Multiply by 40 the number of people already born in Israel when she came to the edge of Canaan the first time around. That's how many personal years of hope deferred have been lived by this nation. In our study of the healing of the condition of deferred hope we will address the issues of the corporate years, recognizing that having addressed corporate issues we will have addressed, as well, issues that belong to the personal years of deferment.

Approaching the end of the closing chapter of the book of Deuteronomy, We have to ask: As Israel camps a second time at the edge of Canaan, with 40 years of wilderness in their bones and mourning the loss of the one who was to lead them into Canaan, what is the condition of the corporate heart? I would venture to say the corporate heart is in need of healing.

Turn the page. The healing is about to begin. Joshua Chapter One….

Make a Note

There are some points we need to make about the process of healing sickness in the heart that comes from long delay of the fulfillment of a God-given hope.

The people of Israel have been here, near Mount Nebo, across the Jordan from Canaan for about two months — one month as Moses worked his way though the Book of Deuteronomy, one month for mourning. And yet nothing moves forward — nothing — and no one sets a foot down in Canaan until God gives specific directions regarding the march into Canaan, as He begins to do in verse two of Joshua Chapter One. Until God speaks, nothing happens.

Point Number One: God Himself initiates the work of healing. God is the initiator — not the circumstances, not the leader. It's not enough to see realization of hope within reach — graspable, if you will. It's not enough to have leaders capable of going into the promise, as Joshua surely was. Men do not initiate, circumstances do not initiate, God Himself must initiate the healing.

Why?

In an earlier chapter we identified the wilderness as a place where things die. All that would hinder us from possessing what God has given falls dead in the wilderness and in that same wilderness there are things born that can and will possess what God has given. Only God knows when everything appointed to die in the wilderness has died, and only God knows when everything appointed to come alive in the wilderness has come alive.

Listen to the words of God: "Moses my servant is dead...Now therefore, arise, go over this Jordan."

Paraphrased: Moses is dead. Now you can go in.

The leader who was to have taken the people into the promise was Himself the last to fall in the wilderness. Because He did not "hallow God in the midst of the children of Israel" (Numbers 20:7-12; 27:12-14), Moses was not permitted to go into Canaan. Once Moses had been buried (by God) and rightly mourned, then and only then did God say, "It's over. The long walk is over. It's time to go into the land."

"Moses my servant is dead."

"...Arise, go over..."

If you will hear this: As Moses was God's servant, so is the wilderness of delay the servant of the living God, Whose thoughts are not like ours. This time of waiting between hope conceived and hope realized is the servant of the Lord. There's a work to be done in this space of time, a work that makes us fit to receive and fit to keep what God wants to give. This time of waiting is the servant through which God does those things that need to be done in us so that we can possess what He has given.

Again, please hear: Our wilderness of deferred hope is the appointed servant of the Most High God. We must not rail against God's appointed servant. Also we must know that the day will come when God sees that what needs to be done has been done — what needs to die is dead, what needs to come alive has come alive — and God will say, "It's over. It's time now to go into the land."

God is the initiator of healing for our hope-sick hearts. That's

Point Number One.

Point Number Two: God initiates the healing by His word, that is to say, He speaks.

Why?

Because God's Word and words are always the issue. We live by the words of His mouth. We live by faith in the words of His mouth, those written down in the Bible and those He speaks to us personally.

See, when God planted that hope in our hearts the issue was the Word and the words of His mouth. Will we receive them? Will we believe them? Will we live by them?

After we've knocked around in the wilderness a while...

After our hearts have been rubbed down, worn down, bruised and wounded...

After we've tasted disappointment and pain...

After we've given up lifting those wings to see if we can fly... When we feel we are shackled to a perch...

The issue is still the Word and the words of His mouth. Will we receive them? Will we believe them? Will we live by them?

That's Point Number Two. God initiates the healing process by the words of His mouth, written and living, because the issue is always His Word.

Point Number Three: Picture this. You've been traipsing around a wilderness. There has been nothing but manna to eat, except for that awful time you had quail coming out your noses. You've been in wars. You've experienced the daily discipline of God. You've witnessed some of the hardest judgments God has to give out. You've lost family members, friends. Many, many thousands of thousands who went with you into the wilderness will never come out of the wilderness. Loss has been your way of life; grief and sorrow, your consistent companions. The worst of it is that you know it's not God's fault, and besides all that, your shoes may not be worn out, but your feet sure hurt.

Now, wouldn't it be nice to hear God say in His softest, most tender voice, "Comfort ye! Comfort ye, My people. I know your sorrow. I know your grief and I've come to soothe your tattered nerves and rub your feet."

Wouldn't it be nice to hear that?

Listen to what God, in fact, says at a time like this. Hear the tone of His voice. Listen to what is said and listen, as well, to what isn't said.

Joshua 1:2, loosely translated: "Moses is dead. It's over. Get up! Get into the land I told you to go into 40 years ago."

The Turks have a saying, "Past, past — future, future!" They say it in Turkish, of course.

The people at the edge of Canaan are in mourning. They are tired. They have suffered loss — much loss. And how does God approach them?

"Past is past. Future is future. Get up and get on with the business I have for you."

This is not the voice of one bringing a pillow and a blanket and hot chocolate for the weary. Sentimentality is conspicuous by its absence. Sympathy's not anywhere around either. There is no allowance for the mental and emotional debris that travels in the wake of years of delay and postponement and loss. Instead comes this call to urgency, this call to action, this call to now action. This is a jarring call — a jarring charge — a jolt — "Get up! Get up now! Go forward!"

Why the jolt? Why the jarring of our souls? You call this healing, Lord?... Sir?

He does.

Think of it as invasive surgery.

Behold the Peanut Butter Jar

Did I mention my jar of peanut butter? Four times I've tried to open it. I've tried brute force. I've tried hot water. I've tried rubber grips. It's the best kind of peanut butter, and I want in that jar. I'm not mad at the jar. I'm not disappointed in the jar. I'm not trying to be difficult about this matter. I just want to get in the jar so I can get out of the jar the good stuff that's in it. The peanut butter jar needs to be invaded. It's time to whack the jar against a solid kitchen counter — Whack! Whack! Whack! That'll knock the seal loose. Whacking works when nothing else will.

There are times when we need to be invaded. We get stuck, just like the lid on the jar of peanut butter. The hope-sickness of our hearts makes us stuck in the way we think. Long seasons of delay, long seasons when the realization of hope is put off, deferred, set aside for the foreseeable future, maybe even beyond the foreseeable future, however long that is — in seasons like that we tend to get stuck in our thinking. We get stuck on hold.

We can't be coaxed out of stuck-on-hold, any more than the lid can be coaxed off that jar of peanut butter. It takes a jolt! It takes a bone-jarring act of God to knock us loose.

'Stuck-on-hold' does not inherit nor can it sustain the promise of God; therefore, God is faithful to provide what is needed. Step one in the process of healing the impact of deferred hope: God comes to us and by His Word and words — whether written in the Bible or direct from His mouth or gift-wrapped in our circumstances and relationships or whatever — He gives us a good, stiff jolt — Whack! Whack! Whack! And it breaks us loose from a mindset that is stuck on hold.

How do we know when our mindset is stuck on hold and this kind of invasive surgery is needed? Stuck-on-hold looks like this.

Diminished Expectation — Flat Emotion

The four leprous men of II Kings 7 are some of my favorite men in the Bible. Their story is a wonderful illustration of the absurd as a strategy of battle. Wonderful as they are, my four heroes suffered from diminished expectation and flattened emotion.

Here they are, sitting at the gate of Samaria. Four men with leprosy. Four men physically sick, socially outcast, religiously unclean, literally rotting away with what was at the time an incurable disease. It is likely that they have been sick, cast out and unclean together for a long time, for it seems that there is among them some kind of friendship, based perhaps on common affliction.

Inside the city of Samaria there is famine. The city has been under siege for a good while. Outside the city of Samaria is the Syrian army. The conversation of our four lepers indicates that they expect nothing good from the Syrian army. In fact, it becomes evident by the conversation of the men that they expect nothing good from any direction at all.

Listen to their words, recorded in II Kings 7:3-4: "Why are we sitting here until we die? If we say, 'We will enter the city,' the famine is in the city, and we shall die there. And if we sit here, we die also. Now therefore, come, let us surrender to the army of the Syrians. If they keep us alive, we shall live; and if they kill us we shall but die."

Translation: "We are dying of leprosy. Why are we sitting here, waiting for death to come. We can get up, go into the city and die of starvation. Or we can sit here and die of leprosy. Let's surrender to the Syrians. If they keep us alive we'll live long enough to die of leprosy and if they kill us...well, we'll only die."

The men have whittled their options to four: (1) They can go into the city and die of starvation. (2) They can sit in the gate and die of leprosy. (3) They can surrender to the Syrians and die of leprosy as prisoners of war. (4) They can surrender to the Syrians and be killed by them, in which case they die.

Diminished expectation: There is no thought expressed that the circumstance in which these men find themselves may improve. There is no consideration given to whether some kind of rescue, supernatural or otherwise, might be at hand. There is only a dull resignation to four grim options. The message is, "We are dead men. Let's choose which way we're going to die."

Flatness of emotion: There is no fear of death. There is no fear of life going on as it is, without change. There is no fear of hunger or of violent death at the hands of the Syrians. There is no anger, justified or otherwise, at the grim lot that is theirs. There is no outcry to God — not even to an idol — for help, for change in the circumstance, for mercy, for comfort, for answers. There is no tenderness toward one another as they contemplate imminent death. There is no self-pity. There is no grieving for what might have been if only this or if only that. There is nothing. There is only the answer of the heart to the decision that must be made, which, translated to contemporary language, goes something like this: "What difference does it make what we do? It's all the same!" Or

"Who cares?" Or "What does it matter?" Or "Whatever."

The four leprous men were stuck on hold, waiting to die. They needed a jolt and God provided one for them. You know the story. Off they went to the Syrian camp, with their flat hearts and their shrinking expectation. The four lepers didn't know it, but God made their eight rotting feet sound like "a noise of chariots and a noise of horses, even the noise of a great host..."

When the men arrived at the camp — Whack! Whack! Whack! — the Syrians had fled, leaving food and wealth behind, enough for the four leprous men and the city of Samaria, too. God's intervention on our behalf can be a pretty stiff jolt when our minds are all made up for death.

Diminished expectation, flatness of emotion. In II Peter 3:4 it sounds like this: "Where is the promise of His coming?...All things continue as they were from the beginning of creation."

In our mouths the words might be, "He promised, but it hasn't happened. Nothing is changed. Everything is just like it was before. It's always been this way. Nothing's ever going to change."

Consider this:

Have you heard these words in your mouth lately? Have you heard them frequently over the past several months or years? When questions have been presented to you in the past month, six months, a year, maybe longer, all kinds of questions, significant questions and insignificant questions, has it been true that most of your answers have been along these lines: "What does it matter" — "What difference does it make?" — "Who cares" — "Whatever."

If so, it may be time to call upon the bone-jarring God. A stiff jolt may be in order.

No Sense of, No Capacity for Urgency

We're stuck on hold when we have lost any sense of urgency about the commands, directives, desires, activity and presence of God, and when we've lost our capacity to move with urgency.

Among the definitions of the word 'urgency' are these words:

the pressure of necessity. The commands, directives and desires of God come with the pressure of necessity, which is not a negative pressure, but, rather, a positive pressure. Because the judgments of God are true and righteous altogether and because He is absolute in His authority, His commands, directives and desires carry a pressure of necessity. If God says it is to be done, then it must be done. No choice. No option. No negotiation. Just do it, and better sooner than later.

In Exodus 20:8-11, God gives command to the children of Israel regarding the Sabbath of the Lord. It is to be kept holy, He says. "In it," He says, "You shall do no work."

In Exodus 31:12-17, the Lord repeats that command and adds that the Sabbath is to be a sign between God and the people of Israel throughout the generations, so that the people of Israel will "know that I am the Lord who sanctifies you."

As well, God commands that anyone who profanes the Sabbath "shall surely be put to death." He says it two times in that passage (31:14-15). Two times in as many verses God points to the severity of punishment assigned to those who profane His Sabbath.

How is it, then, that Numbers 15:32 records the news that "a man was found gathering sticks on the Sabbath day." The man had lost a sense of urgency, was absent the pressure of necessity as regards the commandments of God.

John 20:1-10: Jesus has been crucified. Over and over again, He had told His disciples that He would suffer, would die, would rise again on the third day. Now it is the third day.

"On the first day of the week, Mary Magdalene came to the tomb early and saw that the stone had been taken away from the mouth of the tomb. Then she ran and came to Simon Peter and to the other disciple, whom Jesus loved, and said to them, 'They have taken away the Lord out of the tomb, and we do not know where they have laid Him.'

"Peter therefore went out, and the other disciple, and were going to the tomb. So they both ran together, and the other disciple outran Peter and came to the tomb first. And he, stooping down and looking in, saw the linen clothes lying there; yet he did not go in. Then Simon Peter came, following him, and went into the tomb; and he saw the linen clothes lying there, and the handkerchief that had been around His head, not lying with the linen clothes, but folded together in a place by itself.

"Then the other disciple, who came to the tomb first, went in also; and he saw and believed. For as yet they did not know the Scripture that He must rise again from the dead. Then the disciples went away again to their own homes."

WHAT!!??

The body of their Lord missing, and they went away again to their own homes? What about finding Jesus? Where is He? How is it that His body has disappeared? What about finding the other disciples, taking them to the tomb and saying, "Look! Look at this! There are grave clothes and no body!!" What about telling the people — all the people everywhere — "Jesus said He would rise again and He is not in the tomb! The grave clothes are there, but not the Lord! Have you seen Him? Do you know where He is?"

They went away again to their own homes. Where was the urgent movement regarding the presence of Jesus? Where was the urgent activity in response to the missing body of the Lord?

Earlier in the biography of Jesus of Nazareth, as recorded in Matthew Chapter Two, wise men came from the east, searching for the King of the Jews. They came to worship Him. We're told that Herod was troubled, and rightly so. We're told that all Jerusalem was troubled along with Herod and that the wise men were sent to Bethlehem.

Bethlehem was less than a day's walk from Jerusalem. All Jerusalem was troubled by the report that wealthy, smart men had come a long, long way looking for the King of the Jews, who was to be worshiped. All Jerusalem must have heard at the knees of their parents that the Messiah, Who would be King, was to be born in Bethlehem. After 400 years of silence from God, the news goes out across the city that smart, wealthy men have come a very long way, following a star, to find someone who was born to be King of the Jews. Besides the wealthy, smart men from the east, how many troubled themselves to leave the city of Jerusalem and walk less than a day to get to Bethlehem, to see what they could find. So far as we know, nobody.

Four hundred years of silence. Loss of a sense of urgency, loss of capacity to move with urgency, stuck on hold.

No Intensity Toward God

If we're drained of intensity in regard to the matters of which God has spoken to us, we may be stuck on hold. Definition of intensity: Concentration of energy, force, focus, firm purpose. To be intense is to be undistracted.

Exodus 24:18 ends as Moses climbs Sinai, to talk with God. It was one of many such occasions. We're told that during this visit he was on the mountain 40 days and 40 nights. Moses is busy, making notes. God is pouring out instruction and information. The people at the bottom of the mountain are not so productively occupied.

"Now when the people saw that Moses delayed coming down from the mountain, the people gathered together to Aaron, and said to him, 'Come, make us gods that shall go before us; for as for this Moses, the man who brought us up out of the land of Egypt, we do not know what has become of him'" (Exodus 32:1).

Nor did they care much apparently. The people at the bottom of the mountain had lost energy force, focus and firm purpose in relation to Moses and whatever was going on up there on the mountain. They had become thoroughly distracted. They were ready to party. It should be noted that they were intensely ready to party.

Read again the heading at the beginning of this small section, giving heed to the words, "...drained of intensity in regard to the matters of which God has spoken to us."

Moses was a most intense man. Moses never lost that quality of intensity that so marked him. However, on one very critical occasion Moses did lose intensity in regard to a specific instruction, which God had spoken to him. It cost him his place at the head of the line when the people entered into God's promise. As a matter of fact, it cost him his place in the land, period.

Numbers 20, beginning in verse two. There was no water for

the people of Israel to drink. As usual, the congregation contended with Moses. "If only we had died when our brethren died before the Lord! Why have you brought up the congregation of the Lord into this wilderness, that we and our animals should die here?"

"Take the rod..." the Lord told Moses, "...Speak to the rock ...It will yield its water" (Numbers 20:8).

It soon became evident that Moses was weary of contending with the congregation, so much so that he lost focus and firm purpose in regard to the words of God. Distracted by the anger in his own soul, Moses failed to speak to the rock. Instead, he spoke to the people of God from his place of anger and struck the rock twice. God's response was immediate and severe:

"Because you did not believe Me, to hallow Me in the eyes of the children of Israel, therefore you shall not bring this congregation into the land which I have given them."

Intensity, in and of itself, is not necessarily laudable. However, to retain intensity toward the matters of which God has spoken to us is critical.

At Ease with Loss as a Lifestyle

Loss comes to us in life on planet Earth. Loss especially comes to us in a wilderness of deferred hope. When things die those things are lost to us. Sometimes people that we love are lost to us or people with whom we're comfortable or people upon whom we depend or people that make us feel good. Sometimes possessions of which we've grown fond are lost to us. Sometimes God carves away habits and lifestyles to which we're accustomed or creature comforts or heart attitudes and personality responses that are part of our identity outside the promise of God. Loss comes. Some kinds of loss are more painful than other kinds, but because God is all we need and because He is the more-than-enough God we grow to experience loss gracefully, looking to Him to fill empty spaces and add to us whatever must be added. This is a good thing.

Even so...

Read Deuteronomy 28:1-14. These verses tell of the blessing that comes with obedience to God. It's a story about increase.

Then read Deuteronomy 28:15-68. These verses tell of the curses — call them consequences if you're uncomfortable with the word 'curses' — that come to us when we walk in disobedience. It's a story about loss.

Loss comes. Loss is incurred as God purges us. Purging is pruning. Pruning a tree cleans it up, gets rid of excess, prepares it for increase. This kind of loss is good.

Some loss is robbery and death and is not to be tolerated.

Loss that occurs in the process of purging or pruning gets rid of stuff that will hinder or prevent us from moving in the next place of promise in God. Good riddance to the stuff that is lost! Loss that is robbery and death is to be resisted with all our hearts, souls, minds and strength. In our communion with God we discover, instance by instance, where loss is to be seen as a means to increase and where loss is to be intensely resisted.

Problem: In seasons of long delay we tend to become accustomed to loss. Loss becomes a way of life. We are at ease in a lifestyle of loss when we give no energy to discerning in the presence of God whether loss incurred comes under the heading of pruning, intended to bring increase, or under the heading of robbery and death. We've become at ease with a lifestyle of loss when we simply and passively endure whatever loss comes our way, even counting our passivity a virtue. If we are in such a state our bones need to be jarred.

A 'Tweener' Mentality

We're on hold if we have the heart of a nomad, a consistent and continuing "tweener" mentality. We are always "in between." This does not speak to people who travel or even to people who change their places of residence frequently. Rather this speaks to people who have taken to themselves the soul of a nomad, whether they move frequently, travel or live in one place for an entire lifetime.

Webster's 1828 dictionary defines a nomad as one who leads a wandering life and subsists by tending herds of cattle which graze on herbage of spontaneous growth. It defines wandering as roving or rambling here and there without any certain course or object in view. Spontaneous growth, by Webster's definition, is that which is produced without being planted or without human labor. We can be sojourners, those whose residence — wherever it may be — is temporary, without being wanderers, roving and rambling about without certain course or objective.

Under judgment for the murder of his brother, Cain went to dwell in the land of Nod. The Hebrew word translated 'Nod' is 'nowd.' It describes not exile — though Cain was, indeed, in exile — but rather wandering or vagrancy. It is easy in "wilderness wanderings" to take the heart of a wanderer, to lose sight of the objective that God has set before us, to stray from the course. In 40 years of wilderness walking neither Joshua nor Caleb took the heart of a wanderer. They remembered the objective. They never strayed from the course.

We are workers together with God (II Corinthians 6:1). The clear implication in that statement is that we work. Apart from Christ we can do nothing (John 15:5) — we know it's true. We also know it's true that we will not experience growth and fruitfulness unless energy and effort is expended to plant and to labor. Our faith in the Christ apart from whom we can do nothing is evident in the work that we do. We plant, we sow, we reap that which cannot be produced apart from the power of a supernatural God and will not be produced apart from the labor of our spirits, souls and bodies.

Jesus, the Word of God, said, "You did not choose Me, but I chose you and appointed you that you should go and bear fruit, and that your fruit should remain...Abide in Me, and I in you...for without Me you can do nothing" (John 15:4-5, 16).

The Word of God also says, "...as workers together with Him...work out your own salvation with fear and trembling...All authority has been given to Me in heaven and on earth. Go therefore and make disciples of all the nations, baptizing them in the name of the Father and of the Son and of the Holy Spirit, teaching them to observe all things that I have commanded you...to this end we labor, striving according to His working which works in me mightily...and lo, (Jesus, to Whom all power is given) is with (us) always, even to the end of the age" (II Corinthians 6:1, Philippians 2:12, Matthew 28:18-20, Colossians 1:29).

We do not rove and ramble, nor can we expect to live in a condition of growth without labor. We are not nomads. A nomadic heart is always "in between." Nomads do not cultivate roots nor do they build. They are without sense of ownership and without the responsibility of ownership.

While it is true that we are stewards and not owners of the work of God, it is also true that a good and gracious owner imparts to his stewards something of his own sense of ownership together with the desire for excellence and the sense of responsibility that is a characteristic of fruitful ownership. An excellent steward of the promises of God has an appropriate sense of ownership toward the promise. He knows that he has a place in the promise; he is keen to find his place; and he is strongly desirous to stand in that place.

When we find ourselves functioning as nomads we need a jolt from God.

'Slave' Faith and Energy

We are stuck on hold when we have all the faith and energy of a slave but only the faith and energy of a slave. Slaves work because they have to work. They work for a master they neither choose nor love, and while they do the business of the master, they can be absent of care for the quality of the labor, except as the quality or lack of quality impacts their personal safety, comfort and convenience.

Apart from coercion by a slave owner, slaves simply gather whatever falls at their feet. The most precious things that come from God's don't simply fall at our feet. They are dug out of hard places and somebody has to dig for them. Even for the water in the rock to be released to flow quite freely and abundantly somebody had to do the thing the way God said to do it before the water became available.

The nomad is different from the slave in that the nomad acknowledges no owner while the slave acknowledges an owner, but may not give him honor in the conduct of his (the slave's) life.

Slaves can have lazy bones, resistant bones and resentful bones. Bones that are lazy, resistant and resentful need to be jarred. Nobody does it better than God, and when He has done so, when He has "un-stuck" us, we are in position to receive what He so graciously supplies — the provision for possessing the promise that has been a long time coming.

Chapter 6

The Call for a Leader

Give me a man of God — one man,
True to the vision that he sees,
And I will build your broken shrines
And bring the nations to their knees.
George Liddell

One man true to the vision that he sees. This word 'true'
has an interesting linguistic history. Its Dutch ancestors are
the words 'trouw,' meaning loyalty or fidelity, and 'trouwen,'
meaning to marry. Fidelity is defined as firm adherence to a
person or party with which one is united or to which one is
bound. A second meaning is observance of the marriage covenant.
Loyalty is defined as fidelity to a prince or sovereign or to a husband or lover.

The implications are obvious. We are dead to the law in order
that we might be married to another, even to Him who was raised
from the dead (Romans 7:4), that is, to Jesus, the Prince of Peace
(Isaiah 9:6), Who is absolutely sovereign (Psalm 103:19) and
Whose covenantal book, the Bible, declares that we live by the
words of His mouth (Deuteronomy 8:3, Matthew 4:4). We are
planted together or "united" with Him in death that we might be
in the likeness of His resurrection. Obviously the "uniting" is not
a uniting of essence, for Creator and creature are never one
essence. Rather, we are joined by our position in Him and His in
us (John 14:20). If we are living by the words of His mouth and in

the likeness of His resurrection, then we ought to give evidence of fierce loyalty to the words that He speaks. Such loyalty is an observance of the marriage covenant by our refusal to be separated in purpose and vision from the One to whom we are married.

One man true to his vision. Through such a man God will bring nations to their knees. Maybe George Liddell knew something about God. Maybe he knew that God has always had it in His mind to bring nations to their knees in worship. That's what vision and purpose are all about. That's what it's all about when God deposits hope in us. It's about one more little corner of creation being filled with His glory until the whole earth is full. It's about God being known for Who He is; it's about nations and you and me acknowledging that He is the one true and living God, the Most High God, Who rules over all. It's about all of creation bowing its knee to His gracious and totally righteous government (I Corinthians 15:24-28, Philippians 2:9-11).

That being the case, God has a greater vested interest in fulfillment of hope than we do, and that's a good thing for us.

As we have seen in previous pages, there can be extended periods of time between His communication to us of His vision and purpose — the deposit of hope — and the coming to pass of that vision and purpose. In these extended periods of time our hearts may grow weary and sickly, our thinking may get stuck on hold, we may find ourselves distanced in spirit and soul from hope that was given of God or we may be found sluggish in response to the vision and purpose which we once carried with passion and vigor.

Should we find ourselves in such a condition it is likely that the realization of hope set before us, now clearly within reach, will find us unable to rise to meet the challenge, to take hold of and to possess what God wants to give. The tree of life will be full of fruit; we will be paralyzed in our capacity to eat and enjoy.

God knows our frame that we are dust (Psalm 103:14), and so He brings to our hearts and minds a process of healing in order that the vision and His purpose not be lost. As we saw in Chapter Five, the first step in that healing process is to jar the heart out of its bed of affliction and to break up thinking patterns that are not conducive to seizing the moment. It's like whacking a jar on the edge of a kitchen counter to loosen a stuck lid that gets between us and the good stuff in the jar. A more violent picture, perhaps — it's as if God administers a jolt of electricity to start a heart unwilling or unable to beat as it's supposed to beat.

The second step in the process calls for one good man or woman, depending on the occasion, through whom God can provide a strong focal point of leadership. (Remember, we are addressing corporate concerns, being confident that individuals will make appropriate personal application.)

God and men are always looking for leaders, men *and* women, who in times of delay do not become distanced from the vision and purpose of God. God and men are looking for leaders who will wed themselves to the God of hope and then cling to the words of His mouth through the long passage of time, refusing to be separated from what they have seen and heard. In such men and women are found the qualities necessary to lead disappointed people into their places and positions of appointment.

Maybe George Liddell knew something about God. Maybe he knew that God is always looking for one man true to his vision.

Question is: Why the emphasis on one?

Some thoughts:

I believe in team ministry and service, in the church, in the marketplace and in the home, where husband and wife comprise the leadership team. I also believe that every team has a head, whether we admit it or not, whether we acknowledge it or not. The Bible sets before us the model of teamwork. Every Bible team had a leader, someone who was "out in front."

Twelve men walked closely with Jesus. Twelve men were trained to carry on His work. They were a team. Who was the leader? We would have to say Peter. In the Upper Room the composition of the team shifted slightly. Peter was still the leader.

Barnabas and Saul were a team. Barnabas was the leader. Then Paul moved into the lead and the team became Paul and Barnabas. Either way, the team had a recognized leader. Paul linked up with Silas. Who was the leader of that team? Paul, of course. Moses' father-in-law encouraged Moses to appoint people to help him carry the tasks of leading the people of God. Moses named 70 men, but Moses remained the leader.

David had his mighty men, but David was very clearly the leader, even when he was on the run. Husband and wife are a leadership team; the husband is the leader.

In any team there will be a focal point of leadership. When the people being led are disappointed people, when they're hope-deferred people, when they're people moving into the realization of promise after years of delay, it is even more critical that there be a single and very strong focal point of leadership.

Why?

Three reasons.

First, at that place of movement from delay to realization things may happen very quickly. Long periods of delay often are followed by God's "suddenlies." That's because God's so-called "suddenlies," almost without exception, are the result of extensive preparation and maturation, so that when everything and everyone is rightly positioned there comes what seems to be an explosion of activity that brings into our experience that for which we have only hoped in years past.

When things happen very quickly decisions have to be made very quickly or opportunities can be lost. The decision-making process must be streamlined. The decision-making process is streamlined when there is one very strong focal point of leadership — a man or woman able to hear God, ready to obey and capable of orchestrating good decisions in a timely manner.

Second, leadership is a catalyst. A catalyst is an agent added to a substance, by which a chemical reaction is brought about or speeded up without permanent change occurring in the agent itself.

If I may put it this way: As a catalytic agent Moses was faulty. Having fled from Egypt as a young man, after murdering an Egyptian, and having spent 40 years tending another man's sheep on the backside of the desert, Moses returned to Egypt, to be added to the people of Israel. He was to be a catalyst. By word and action during the next 40-plus years Moses provoked the reactions and responses necessary to get the people out of Egypt through the wilderness and to the edge of the promised land — twice. Moses, however, did not remain unchanged by the substance to which he was added. The long walk with a rebellious people stirred in Moses a response that did not "hallow" God in the sight of the people whom he (Moses) led. Moses misrepresented God in his place of responsibility. The error cost him his place in the promise.

It is twice said in the Book of Deuteronomy (1:38 and 31:7) that Joshua will cause Israel to inherit the land. The Hebrew word translated 'cause' (KJV) is 'dhavar' or 'dabar' in the 38th verse of chapter one and 'nathan' in the seventh verse of chapter 31. 'Dhavar' speaks of words; 'nathan' essentially means to give or to put something in or on a place, to fasten something in place.

God found in Joshua a man who walked 40 years with the children of Israel and remained unchanged — that is to say, Joshua had seen the God of the promise and he had seen the promise; he knew where Israel was going; he was determined to get there. God had found an effective catalyst. Joshua was added as a leader to the people of Israel, and by his words — presumably such words as he received from God — Joshua was to bring about reactions, responses and decisions that would set Israel in its place, that would fasten Israel in the place to which they were appointed.

To walk among society as a catalyst, undistracted from the purpose of God, provoking reactions and responses that establish His purpose, yet remain unchanged by the society in which one walks demands extraordinary strength of character and focus of heart and mind. God looks for men and women of this quality to bring His people out of delay into fulfillment. Paul, Peter, Barnabas in his time, and yes, Deborah of the Book of Judges (chapters four and five) — these were such people, team players, but very clearly the focal points of leadership.

Third, the leader of a community is what we might call a "gate" into that community. Things come in and things go out of a community through a gate. While there are many such openings in communities, the role of the leader of any entity — state, city, church, family, a team of workers — makes that particular "gate" an especially critical entrance or exit for at least two reasons. One of those reasons has to do with a leader's position as a catalyst, someone who sparks reactions and responses that further the purposes of God. The second reason relates to the leader's place in the flow of delegated governmental authority. As a representative of God, a leader is to bring to the community God's blessing and the order of His government.

God commended Abraham, the head of his family and the father of nations, as one who would "command his children and his household after him," that they "would keep the way of the Lord" (Genesis 18:19).

In the patriarchs Isaac and Jacob (later named Israel) we see very clearly the authority of the head of the community to pronounce blessing over the community, and in so doing to release the provision, the favor, the positioning and the correction of God (Genesis 27 and 49). We see that same kind of authority exercised through Moses as blessing is released into the nation of Israel (Deuteronomy 33).

We see a whole nation called to account for the covenant-breaking action of King Saul, even many years after the covenant was violated, and we see King David addressing that action on behalf of the nation he ruled, thereby bringing to the nation relief from three years of famine (II Samuel 21).

We see all Jerusalem troubled with Herod, their ruler, who is distressed at the news that the King of the Jews has been born (Matthew 2). Later, we see murder released into a nation as Herod, in rage and fear, kills all the male children of Bethlehem, two years old and under.

We see husbands, as leaders in the home, commanded to love their wives, even as Christ loved the Church, to release into the lives of their wives the same nurture and care that they would give their own bodies (Ephesians 5:25-29).

In I Peter 3:7 we discover that a husband's disregard for the honor of his wife will hinder his own prayers and by extrapolation hinder the release of God's blessing to the home.

Leaders are gates into communities. Things come in gates and things go out of gates; blessing or cursing can be allowed in or kept out at gate places. It is incumbent upon leaders to let God-things into the community and keep out of the community not-God-things.

When God prepares a community to lay hold of a promise that has been long delayed, a strong, single focal point of leadership makes for a narrower gate. It makes for an entry point and place of exit that is more tightly restrictive and more discriminating. These are good qualities for critical gates.

> Give me a man of God — one man
> True to the vision he sees
> And I will build your broken shrines,
> And bring the nations to their knees.

At the edge of Canaan, after the death of Moses, God called for Joshua.

Chapter 7

Some Die – Some Dig In

"...By my God have I leaped over a wall."
Psalm 18:29

It was an early-morning prayer meeting. The sun was not yet up, the sleep not entirely gone from our eyes or our minds. Perhaps, we considered, that's why she mis-remembered and, so, misquoted over and over again, the Scripture we'd just finished reading. It was not a large departure from the words on the page. Essentially, she was saying the same thing the words on the page were saying. However, after the verse had been misquoted a few times and when the sleep had cleared from our minds, it occurred to us that the "mis-speak" very well could be a God-thing. The words on the page read: "...by my God have I leaped over a wall." The lady was saying, "...by my God have I vaulted over a wall."

To leap is to move oneself suddenly from the ground by using one's leg muscles. To vault is to jump, leap or spring, as over a barrier or from one position to another, especially with the help of the hands supported on the barrier or holding a long pole. The one who vaults uses the pole, first, to dig into the ground and then, by the spring in the pole, to give momentum to what would be without the pole a very ordinary leap. The misquoting prayer warrior pointed out: One who vaults must first dig in.

'To vault' was the term better suited to the circumstance about which we were praying at the time. It is the term better suited, as well, to describe Joshua's journey through the wilderness alongside the people of Israel. What was required of Joshua was no "ordinary leap." What was required of him was an extraordinary vault. If Joshua's hands had any "wall" to grip in order to make that 40-year vault, it was the small walk he'd had in the land promised. If he had any "pole" it was what he had seen and what he knew of his God:

"The land we passed through to spy out is an exceedingly good land," Joshua had said. "If the Lord delights in us, then He will bring us into this land and give it to us, a land which flows with milk and honey.

"Only do not...fear the people of the land, for they are our bread; their protection has departed from them, and the Lord is with us. Do not fear them" (Numbers 14:7-9).

Joshua gripped with his hands and dug in with his pole and God threw a mantle of leadership around his shoulders.

There's something we must know about leaders. Leaders are more than people who impart information, more than givers of instruction, more than issuers of directions and commands, more even than servants, although servants they must be.

I Peter 5:2-3 says this to leaders: "Shepherd the flock of God which is among you, serving as overseers, not by constraint but willingly, not for dishonest gain but eagerly; nor as being lords over those entrusted to you, but being examples to the flock..."

It's this word 'examples' I'd like for us to hear. The Greek word is 'tupos.' It speaks of a mark or an impression made by striking something. It would be as if we took a very soft piece of clay — or even a fairly resistant piece of clay — and struck it with a wooden initial, perhaps yours, perhaps mine, leaving in the clay a clear impression of a large letter 'A' or perhaps an 'S,' depending on whose initial we used. The impression of the letter left in the clay is a 'tupos.'

If we were to squarely and solidly and deliberately set one of our bare feet down in soft, rich, maybe very black soil and then pick it up again, the clear impression of a bare foot left in the soil is a 'tupos.'

A leader is someone who is pressed into the life of another, or many others, and by the pressure or by the "pressing in" of his presence and participation in that life, by the weight of his own life lived out before his followers — or even, follower, singular — there is left a clear and identifiable mark, a clear and identifiable impression.

We don't know much about Joshua's life in Egypt, as a very young man. From Numbers 13 we can know that he was a ruler, or a leader, among the people of the tribe of Ephraim. Joshua first appears in the Bible in Exodus 17:9, when Moses speaks to him, saying, "Choose us some men and go out, fight with Amalek."

In verse 13 of Exodus Chapter 17 it is recorded that Israel defeated Amalek, with Joshua himself leading the battle. In verse 14 the Lord instructs Moses to "...write this for a memorial in the book and recount it in the hearing of Joshua, that I will utterly blot out the remembrance of Amalek from under heaven."

The evidence of the passage suggests that Joshua is going to be a significant person in the history of the nation.

In Chapter 24 of Exodus we learn that Joshua became a servant to Moses, but so much more than a servant, and Moses, so much more than a master. Moses became a mentor to Joshua. He became to Joshua what Joshua himself would become to the Israelites, a 'tupos.'

Forty years in the wilderness. We can be sure that Joshua, running at the heels of Moses, was not draped daintily across the surface of the people of Israel like a piece of fine lace. We can be sure that Joshua lived the daily-ness of the nation he would eventually lead.

We can be sure that Joshua, as he lived out the daily-ness of the wilderness, was pressed into the lives of the people, with the divine intent that he leave a mark or an impression in their souls. We can be sure he was pressed into the soil of their hearts, even as a seed would be pressed into the earth.

Forty years in the wilderness. Joshua did more than survive. He came out of the wilderness a conqueror. The question would be, what was the nature of this man Joshua that God found so very malleable? Who was this 'tupos' God had chosen to lead His disappointed, delayed people in their wars of possession?

Again, the evidence of Scripture.

A Man of Radical Obedience

Joshua was a man who lived by the words of the mouth of God. He was a man of radical obedience.

Radical speaks of the root of a matter. Joshua was obedient down to the root. The word 'radical' speaks of that which is fundamental. Joshua was a man whose fundamental character was one of obedience to God.

On the strength of God's promise, Joshua endured 40 years of hard judgment incurred because of somebody else's unbelief. He lived daily with the consequences of somebody else's sin. He was aware daily of the fruit of disobedience, that is to say, he was aware daily of the death and devastation that comes of unbelief. He knew the cost of disobedience. He wasn't interested in paying it.

I've wondered sometimes, why didn't he ever make a break for it; make a mad dash to somewhere — maybe in the direction of Canaan — just to see how far he could get. He didn't make a break for it because the promise of God was for the nation. He was part of the nation. God said the nation would wander until all the unbelief was dead. God was bringing up a new generation, and Joshua figured God was worth waiting for.

Joshua's radical obedience would be essential in the conquest of Canaan, from which the previous inhabitants were being evicted because of their great wickedness. As Joshua was radically obedient, so the nations of Canaan were radically disobedient, wicked to the root. It's necessary that we understand: Radical disobedience will be challenged successfully only by radical obedience.

Joshua was a man who could challenge radical disobedience. He walked the 40 years because God had decreed the 40 years. He walked it for the hope, for the promise, for the words from the mouth of God who cannot lie.

Against the Flow

Joshua could swim upstream when the purpose of God made it necessary to do so. Numbers chapters 13 and 14 recount the mission of 12 rulers, one from each of the 12 tribes of Israel, sent ahead of the nation into Canaan. God already had given them the land. The assignment of the 12 men was to figure out which route Israel should take to victory. Ten of those 12 men took a look at the land and the people and the cities and reported, upon returning from the mission: "Victory is not in our future; we can't take the land!"

Two of them, Joshua and Caleb, gave a different report. "God is with us," they said. "We can do it."

Nearly the entire nation rejected the report of Joshua and Caleb. Aligning themselves instead with the 10, Israel lifted up a common voice and complained and wept and cried out, "Let's go back to Egypt!"

With Caleb, Joshua said, "Don't rebel against the Lord. The protection of Canaan is gone. The Lord is with us."

When those weeping, complaining people set out to stone Joshua (and Caleb, too), Joshua stood his ground, right where God said to stand. Joshua could swim upstream, not only against the current of popular opinion, but against the barrage of external circumstances and events. He had walked the same land the 10 despairing spies had walked. He had seen the same cities, the same walls, the same giants. In his ears God's promise spoke more loudly than anything else. In his eyes God's promise was bigger, weightier, more real than the external evidence.

Seeing What God Sees

Ten spies saw walls too high, cities too fortified, giants too giant. Joshua saw what God saw. The land was a good land. There was milk and honey in it and big grapes, and a people called Canaanites who'd lost their nerve, and, of course, there was a God Who had said, "This is what I want done."

Joshua saw what God saw. In God, you know, this is what vision is all about. It's about being able to see something of what God sees because He's shown it to you and because He's called you to be a worker together with Him as He brings the thing into time and space.

Without vision, without being able to see something of what God sees, we perish. To perish — Proverbs 29:18 — is the Hebrew word 'para.' It means to let go, to dismiss oneself from the work, to reject, to be unruly, to be unbridled, to be lawless. The sense of the word is to let something slip through the fingers by ignoring an opportunity. Sounds like the people of Israel to me.

Remembering the Taste of the Fruit

Joshua had walked the land, helped carry the grapes back to camp. No doubt, he grazed a bit on the good fruit and the milk and the honey while he was there, spying. Key thought: Joshua remembered what he had seen and tasted and heard. The up-and-down, round-about, in-and-out roller coaster rides we experience — whether in the emotions or in the spirit or in matters of determination and persistence — these moments come because we have short memories. In the moment when God comes to surround us, to speak to us, to plant in us a seed called hope — in that moment we taste, we hear, we see. But we forget the taste, the view and the sound of the Lord, and so we waiver, maybe even let go, dismiss ourselves from the work, reject the plan, let some opportunity slip through our fingers.

Mark 6:45-52: The Lord's disciples, in a boat in the midst of a storm, saw Jesus quiet the storm. They were astounded and amazed not because they'd never seen a miracle, but because they failed to consider the miracle that immediately preceded the storm, the miracle of the loaves, the feeding of the multitudes with somebody's little lunch. They didn't understand. Maybe they didn't understand because they didn't remember (Mark 8:14-21). Joshua remembered.

A Confidence Earned

One more time! Joshua walked every step of the 40 years in the wilderness, right along with all the people who would die and, even more significantly, right along with all the ones growing up, the ones who would follow him across the Jordan into Canaan.

Again, that long walk was the consequence of somebody else's sin. It was a judgment on somebody else's unbelief, but if Joshua complained about his lot it's not recorded. If he whined we don't hear about it. If he had moments of rebellion we're not told. Joshua did what was necessary to do, what was his to do, and in the doing of it he earned the trust and confidence of the people with whom he walked.

In the first chapter of the Book of Joshua, responding to Joshua's initial instructions regarding the march into Canaan, the people of Israel proclaimed: "All that you command us we will do, and wherever you send us we will go."

I have a friend. We have been friends since the early days of our walk with God. In those early days we met at 5 a.m. every Saturday, at a breakfast place in the city in which we lived. Every Saturday we spent several hours, always more than two, reading the Word of God together, meditating (aloud, of course) on what we'd read, discovering the Lord together.

Later, we both moved to the same small town. Though our moves were not simultaneous, they were not far separated in time. Just as we had in the city, we discovered the Lord together, there in that small town. Then our paths separated geographically.

Some months after the paths divided, as we were talking together on the phone, as we were finding that our hearts were still synchronized in their rhythms, my friend made this comment: "I have lots of new friends. I like my new friends. They're good friends. But I have a history with you."

There's something about people who have a history together. Joshua and the people of Israel had a common history and, therefore, there was a common heart with a common rhythm.

For quite some time I've been intrigued by the words of I Peter 5:1: "…The elders who are among you…" Not all elders, not all leaders, are among the people. Some stay a little bit off to the side. Some hover above. Some stay in front. Some linger behind. There are elders, however, who are among us. They live the daily-ness with us. They make a history with us. Joshua was such a man.

Keeping an Edge

Joshua was able to maintain an edge in a time of long delay.

He retained his sense of urgency and his capacity to respond to urgent issues. In war, he was ready for war (Exodus 17). When God's presence was to be sought and found, Joshua was ready to find it (Exodus 33:11). If it became necessary for him to be corrected, he was ready to receive correction (Exodus 32:17-18, Numbers 11:27-29).

We don't find Joshua picking up sticks on the Sabbath or complaining about Moses or taking forbidden spoil from battle and hiding it in his tent. Joshua kept himself in position to receive whatever God wanted to give at any moment. He maintained his sense of urgency and his capacity to act with appropriate urgency.

A sense of urgency, we have said before, has less to do with time than it does with priority. Joshua's priority was the God of the promise, and Joshua kept himself rightly positioned in that priority. When it came time for the nation to enter the land of Canaan, Joshua intended to be ready and fully qualified for entry, no matter how long he had to wait.

Luke 12:39-40 gives an important instruction related to urgency. Earlier verses admonish us to be like men whose master is expected to return from a wedding. Such men, obviously servants, would be watching carefully in order to open the door to the master when he comes. The Bible says:

"...Know this, that if the master of the house had known what hour the thief would come he would have watched and not allowed his house to be broken into. Therefore you also be ready, for the Son of Man is coming at an hour you do not expect."

Joshua was a "house" that would not be broken into. He was watching for the God of the promise to show up. He was alert. He maintained his readiness. Joshua was a man who kept his edge. The capacity to maintain a sense of urgency comes, at least in part, from a capacity to focus on the main issue or issues of one's life. Joshua had that capacity.

Radical Focus

Joshua was single-minded. Joshua had an eye that was single. Again, the word 'radical' speaks of root issues. To the very root of his nature Joshua had one goal — the destination God had set

Some Die — Some Dig In

95

before him and before the Israelites. The importance of every
other person, thing or circumstance was measured by its position
relative to that one goal.

We can see this kind of focus in Joshua as he encounters the
Lord Himself, just before the first battle of Canaan, at Jericho
(Joshua 5:13). Alone, near the city, Joshua "lifted his eyes and
looked" and there stood a Man, with a sword drawn in His hand.
Joshua had only one question for this Man: "Are you for us or for
our adversaries?" Paraphrased Joshua was asking the Man this
question: Where do you fit in this matter of possessing the land?

Whatever dealing Joshua was going to have with this Man, the
nature of it was going to hinge on the answer to that question. Joshua
understood something about vision. He understood something
about hope when God puts it in us. He understood something
about divinely ordained goals. Everything in our lives is to be
measured by that divinely ordained goal, that hope, that vision:
Does this person, thing or circumstance bring me closer to living
by the words of God's mouth, words that have been entrusted to
me? Or does this person, thing or circumstance constitute a distraction from the purpose of God?

And, by the way, in many instances we need a word from God
to answer the question rightly. Things, after all, are not always as
they seem.

This particular encounter between the Lord and Joshua gives
a clue to another aspect of Joshua's character, something that is
also necessary in a leader, particularly when that leader is leading
disappointed people.

Clarity in Relationship

Two issues here — one of simple relationship, one of relationship as it figures in the vision God has given.

Confronted as he was, in the fifth chapter of the Book of
Joshua, by this "Man with a sword drawn in His hand," Joshua
wasted no time trying to guess where this Man stood in relationship to the people of Israel. He asked the direct question: Are you
for us or against us?

That's issue number one, simple relationship. Friend or foe, it's good to be able to identify who's who.

The second issue that must be clear in relationship is whether I have a common vision with this person to whom I am joined. If we're going to walk together very closely or for a great distance then it's necessary that we be found pursuing the same words from the mouth of God, or at least words that are compatible. The Book of Amos asks, "Do two walk together without having agreed to do so?" Can they agree to walk together if they're walking on extremely divergent paths?

Peter and Paul were, both of them, on God-paths. Both paths were laid out by God, but they took Peter and Paul in different directions — Peter in the direction of the Jews, Paul to the Gentiles. You and I may be walking on different paths, both of which may be God-paths, but you and I must find and walk most closely with the ones whom God has appointed to the paths we're on.

Joshua had a propensity for clarity in relationship. Earlier in the account of Joshua's life, his desire for clarity in relationship placed him in need of correction. The story is told in Numbers 11. The Lord has instructed Moses to gather 70 men of the elders of Israel, men upon whom God intended to send something of the Spirit that was upon Moses, something of the Spirit of God. These 70 men were to help Moses bear the weight of the business of government.

So Moses called the 70 to the tabernacle of meeting, outside the camp of the Israelites. However, two of the 70 stayed behind, inside the camp. When the Spirit of God came, He came on all 70 — the 68 outside the camp and the two inside the camp — and all 70 began to prophesy.

Now, that just didn't seem right to Joshua. After all the men outside the camp, at the tabernacle of meeting, were where they were supposed to be. The men who'd stayed behind, inside the camp, were not where they were supposed to be...so what was the Spirit of God doing resting on people who were not where they were supposed to be? It bothered Joshua that the prophesying going on among the men who were in the right place would slop over on the men who were in the wrong place.

Joshua registered his protest: "Moses my lord, forbid them (to prophesy)" (Numbers 11:28).

"Oh, Joshua," Moses responded (in paraphrase), "are you zealous for my sake? Would that all the Lord's people were prophets and that the Lord would put His Spirit upon them all!"

A reminder for us: Clarity in relationship, in function, in order and arrangement is a good thing, but this God of ours sometimes slops over on stuff outside what we would define as clarity. We must learn to recognize it when it happens, and we must learn to honor it when it happens.

Seeing Life

It couldn't have been encouraging, that 40-year hike. Death was everywhere. Friends were dying; relatives dying; distant acquaintances dying; rumors of death among people even more distant in relationship. Everywhere, death. I can't prove this by Scripture, but I'm sure Joshua had a capacity to see death everywhere and look beyond, to the life coming up.

Knowing that he would go into the promise of God shoulder to shoulder with this growing generation, Joshua must have been a careful observer of people. As the generation came to maturity, I'm sure he made note of their strengths and weaknesses, their gifts and abilities. I'm sure he watched them discover God, remembering all the while, "These are the ones who, with Caleb and myself, will enter the land."

It is necessary that a leader's eye be more attuned to life than to death, even when there's death everywhere and signs of life seem minimal. I was walking down a dirt road in the country one day when a flash of brilliant color off to the left of the road caught my attention. I paused in my walk, to find the source of that sudden flash of color. On a tree just off the road to the left, I saw one, single leaf of brilliant tones, copper, red and gold. I stepped to the side of the road and reached out to touch the color. It was so very beautiful! Carefully, so as not to tear the leaf from the tree, I turned the leaf over and over in my hand, viewing the color from every angle and in every turn of light and shadow. And then the voice of the Lord came.

"What are you doing?"

It seemed obvious what I was doing, but I answered politely, "I'm looking at this leaf, Lord."

"Why?" He asked.

"Because the color is so beautiful, and I wanted to see it close up and appreciate it fully."

"Look all around that leaf," came the response. "What do you see?"

I did as I was told, and I saw green leaves. There were actually lots and lots of green leaves all around the bright copper-red-gold one, and there was brought to my mind a biology lesson learned in some classroom, somewhere, many years before.

I'd learned that leaves change colors because they're dying. I'd been stopped in my walk and drawn away from my course by the look of death, by the attention-demanding colors of death in the tree. I'd failed to notice even briefly the bright green of life everywhere, all over the tree.

Another question came.

"Why are you looking at death when there is life all around to be seen?"

We see death easily. To see life is sometimes harder for us. It shouldn't be. I don't think it was for Joshua. I think Joshua set his eyes on life coming up all around him, because that growing-up generation was evidence from God that the promise had not been lost, had not been taken away, that the land was yet before them and was yet theirs for the taking.

A Good Decision-maker

Hear Noah Webster's definition of decisive: "Having the power or quality of determining a question, doubt or any subject of deliberation; final conclusive, putting an end to controversy."

People who have been wandering around in some pattern of circles — internally if not externally — for 40 years are not likely to have good decision-making skills. A people whose mindset is stuck on hold is not likely to possess a corporate decisiveness. Disappointed people are not likely to make clean, clear, timely decisions. Hope-deferred people need a leader who can do so.

Joshua was such a leader. He made clean, clear, timely decisions, though they were not always right decisions. Consider his decision regarding the sound wafting up from the camp as he and Moses came down from Sinai (Exodus 32). Their long stay on the mountain was too much delay for this restless, fresh-out-of-Egypt people. They turned their gold into a calf and partied hearty.

When Joshua heard the shouting of the people he decided quickly — there's war in the camp. Moses, older and wiser and more experienced, quickly corrected him, "It is not the voice of them that shout for mastery, neither is it the voice of them that cry for being overcome: but the noise of them that sing do I hear."

Or consider his decision regarding the two men who prophesied inside the camp when the other 68 appointed to be elders were prophesying outside the camp. "Make them stop, Moses!" Again, Moses corrected his protege. Joshua's quick decisions were not always good ones.

But also consider Joshua's stand at the edge of the promised land, in the sight of all Israel, people who were quite ready to stone him for that stand: "It's a good land!" Joshua insisted. "We can do it if God is pleased with us! Do not rebel against the Lord, and do not fear the people of the land. Their defense has departed from them and the Lord is with us."

Consider, too, that it was Joshua who chose the men and led the men and carved out the battle strategy that gave the resounding victory against the Amalekites, Israel's first war experience as a free people. Successful warriors are effective decision-makers.

Consider that it was Joshua who decided to send into Jericho two spies instead of 12, as were sent across the Jordan the first time — not so many voices, not so much opportunity for confusion as to the nature of the battle ahead. Good decision-making.

Consider that the decision-making task of distributing inheritance in the land fell to Joshua. All the matters of who gets what, how much goes to whom, and what do you do with inheritance when there are no sons but only daughters in the family.

And consider Joshua's statements recorded in Joshua 24:14-15: "Now therefore fear the Lord, and serve Him in sincerity and in truth: and put away the gods which your fathers served on the other side of the flood, and in Egypt, and serve ye the Lord. And if it seem evil unto you to serve the Lord, choose you this day whom ye will serve; whether the gods which your fathers served that were on the other side of the flood, or the gods of the Amorites, in whose land ye dwell: but as for me and my house, we will serve the Lord."

Don't mistake, please, what I'm about to say. In the Lord, decisions are important and they must be carefully made, but there is room for error. All decisions are acts of faith. We make the best decisions we can make with the information we have and then we trust the Lord to revise, correct, overcome or set aside as may be necessary.

I am reminded of a story about a highly respected, very successful military leader wisely noted for his decision-making abilities. In battle matters he made clear, clean decisions very quickly and seemed to suffer little from undue concern as to whether the decisions were right or wrong. When asked the secret of his ability to make rapid, fearless decisions he answered, "I know that if I've made a wrong decision, if I've designed a plan that won't work, or made a grave error in judgment, someone somewhere down the line will correct the decision I've made."

In the context of faith: We are free to make decisions that are acts of faith. We are free to make clear, clean decisions in a timely manner, knowing that if we have made a wrong decision, Somebody up the line, namely God, will correct the decision we've made in faith.

No Carbon Copy

Numbers 27:18, 20: "And the Lord said to Moses, Take thee Joshua, the son of Nun, a man in whom is the spirit, and lay thine hand upon him; ...And thou shalt put some of thine honor upon him, that all the congregation of the children of Israel may be obedient."

Honor can be seen as that which causes us to know who is Joe and who is Sam and who is George. It's a recognition issue. Some of the honor of Moses was put on Joshua — not all of it. Some of what Joshua had was what Moses had. Some of what Joshua had was all Joshua's from God.

It's important to know: Carbon-copy people don't make good leaders.

God didn't clone Moses in order to produce a Joshua. God gave Joshua to Moses, who trained Joshua and who laid hands on Joshua and who imparted to Joshua some of the honor that had been on him. The rest of whatever Joshua needed in the way of honor Joshua had to get straight from God Himself.

People are born different from one another. Leaders are people; therefore, leaders are born different from one another. Isaac was Abraham's son. Though he repeated some of his father's mistakes (Compare Genesis 20 with Genesis 26:6-12), he was not exactly like Abraham. Jacob was not like Isaac, nor was he like Joseph. Joseph and Moses led nations, but Moses and Joseph were more not alike than they were alike, and neither one of them was like Samuel or Paul or Peter or John. What each of these leaders had in common was that each was chosen of God for a specific task and a specific place in God's kingdom. Different tasks, different qualities needed, different people needed.

We get some understanding, some wisdom, some practical training, some habits (good and bad) from those who've gone before us, from those who teach us, from those who train us, but we're not called to be exactly like any one of these people. We're called to be what God created us to be and what He then makes us to be by the specific shaping work of His hands. That's how Joshua got to be Joshua: He was hand-crafted. Every good leader is hand-crafted by God.

Chapter 8

Work Zone: Leader in the Making

*"The final test of a leader is that he
leaves behind him in other men
the conviction and the will to carry on..."*
Walter Lippman
"Roosevelt Has Gone"
April 10, 1945

Imagine with me:
Silently Moses gazes at the expanse of land stretching itself
out beyond the river. He is able to see much more than he could
have expected to see had not the Lord been there with him, show-
ing him, allowing him to look west, north, south and east to the
vast regions of ground, which his feet would never touch. As he
sees, he remembers.

As human events are reckoned, it was the worst thing that
could have happened to Moses. They were together, he and Aaron,
standing before a thirsty and impatient congregation. Moses had
received his instruction from God: Take the rod, speak to the rock,
it will yield its water (Numbers 20:8).

But when Moses had lifted the rod, just as he had been told to
do, all the anger found its way out. It was much stronger than he
had imagined, and he had heard himself saying, "Hear now, you
rebels! Must we bring water for you out of this rock?" (Numbers
20:10).

The words were not entirely gone from his mouth when he

swung the rod and struck the rock, not once but twice.

God's verdict had been swift in coming.

"Because you did not believe Me, to hallow Me in the eyes of the children of Israel, therefore you shall not bring this congregation into the land which I have given them" (Numbers 20:12).

So then... Moses himself would be among the dead left behind in the wilderness.

Only once had Moses dared to ask the Lord to consider again.

"Oh, Lord God," he had cried out, "You have begun to show Your servant Your greatness and Your mighty hand, for what god is there in heaven or on earth who can do anything like Your works and Your mighty deeds? I pray, let me cross over and see the good land, beyond the Jordan, those pleasant mountains and Lebanon" (Deuteronomy 3:24-25).

God's answer was abrupt: "Speak no more to Me of this matter" (Deuteronomy 3:26).

However, by the Lord's mercy, Moses would not die until he had stood on Pisgah and looked across the Jordan into the land.

And so now he stands silent, looking from Pisgah on Mount Nebo to the regions beyond the river, wondering at the wide reach of land God has given, stunned by the beauty of it.

The Lord speaks softly, for He is very near His servant.

"This is the land of which I swore to give Abraham, Isaac, and Jacob, saying, 'I will give it to your descendants.' I have caused you to see it with your eyes, but you shall not cross over there" (Deuteronomy 34:4).

Abraham... Isaac... Jacob... and now it is time. Moses sighs heavily. Suddenly very tired, he lowers himself to the ground. He is speaking to his God now, about Joshua.

The Measure of Leadership

The measure of the leadership of the man called Moses is not found in the final few moments of his life, alone with His God, on Mount Nebo. It's not found in a grave in a valley in the land of Moab, where God buried His servant. These moments and places are the memorials of his humanity. Nor is his leadership to be measured by the weeping and mourning of the children of Israel as they honored the life in time and space of the one who had walked at their head for more than 40 years of the nation's history and who had carried the nation in his heart for many more years than that.

At least to some significant degree, the measure of the leadership of Moses is found in the man Joshua, into whom Moses had pressed his fingerprint. Some of what had been in Moses was in Joshua. God had determined that it should be so. Moses was the 'tupos.' He was the example/teacher chosen for Joshua. There can be no denying that our teachers leave deep impressions in our souls and in our spirits. As instruments of God, they help to build the fires in which character is forged.

We have seen Joshua as a man who lived by the words of God's mouth; who could hold his direction when the current of human pressure was running another course; who could see the things that God could see; who, when his mouth was dry and the road was long, could remember the good taste of God's promise. He was a man who experienced the consequences of somebody else's sin, without complaining; he was a man who stayed in position to receive the reward of God whenever and however it might come. He was a man of decision, a man who could see life in the midst of death, a man who insisted upon clarity in his relationships and he was a man of radical focus. As well, Joshua was just that...he was Joshua. He was himself and not a carbon copy.

It's men of this fabric who are needed when it's time to lead a people out of disappointment. On what anvils are such men hammered out? Consider these:

The Anvil of War

It is unlikely that Joshua entered the wilderness as a raw recruit in matters of concern to warriors, but it is very likely that he came to view war from a different perspective as he followed God through the wilderness. For those who would walk after the Captain of the Lord's Hosts, war is primarily a supernatural encounter between the warrior and his God.

The lesson of the Red Sea could not have been lost on Joshua. Israel was caught between an impassable body of water and the raging pursuit of the armies of Pharoah, for whom a nation of slaves was no match at all. Any reasonable military leader with care for his people would have recognized the options: Surrender and hope for the best or engage in a battle lost before it begins, thus resigning yourself to massive casualties and inevitable captivity for any who may survive such an engagement.

If, however, you happen to have in hand a rod of God there is an alternative. Ask God what to do; do what He says to do; and revel in His salvation.

Joshua's mentor had a rod of God in his hand. He stretched it out over the impassable body of water and the body of water became very passable indeed, dry land even. Pharoah's armies had no rod of God. When the Egyptians followed the Israelites across the floor of the Red Sea, the waters closed over them, every one of them, horses and chariots, too. End of battle. Time for Israel to dance and sing.

Then there was the battle with the Amalekites at Rephidim, a word which means, interestingly enough, 'supports' (in one of its translations). Here is the strategy: Joshua chooses warriors, leads the battle. Moses takes Aaron and Hur and the rod of God and goes to the top of a hill overlooking the field of battle. When he lifts his hand with the rod of God, Israel wins; when he lets his hands down, Amalek wins. That's why Aaron and Hur are on the hill. When Moses' arms become weary, Aaron adds support to one arm; Hur adds support to the other. Israel wins. Simple.

There were other kinds of wars that came to the people of God. There were wars with hunger and ugly temper (Exodus 16, Numbers 16). God's strategy came in supernatural supply and with vindication. There were wars with thirst and ugly temper (Exodus 15:22-24). God's strategy came by way of supernatural activity (Exodus 15:25-26). There were wars with rebellion in the hearts of people and ugly temper (Numbers 12, 14, 16). God's strategy was supernatural judgment.

There were and there are all kinds of wars in which God's people engage. There were and there are all kinds of supernatural strategies from a supernatural God for every kind of enemy and all manner of temper.

We are formed in war by three elements: Our response to war, the supernatural supply of God for our need in the war and our response to the nature of His attention to the need.

The end of war, its purpose, is our growing recognition of and reliance on the strategies of God. The strategies of God, received at His mouth in the immediacy of war, are in every way different from strategies we might concoct ourselves.

The end of war is our embrace of His faithfulness, our grip on unshakable confidence in the truth of His Word and our discovery and re-discovery of the raw force of obedience.

The end of war is that we find rest in the safety of our hiding place in the power of His arm.

The study of war under God is critical to the formation in us of the thought processes of God. So critical is the study that when Israel came into its inheritance God deliberately left in their land occasion for war. He deliberately did not drive out five rulers of the Philistines and their people, all the Canaanites, the Sidonians and the Hivites. The Word of God tells us (Judges 3:1-4) that God calculatedly left these nations in the land "so that the children of Israel might be taught to know war, at least those who had not formerly known it" and "to test Israel by (the nations) to know whether they would obey the commandments of the Lord."

When we walk with God, war comes. Internal wars come from our own appetites and drives. External wars come with people, with circumstances, with the enemy of God. In a fallen world, war comes. God is looking for a particular response, one Joshua-like in tone, something along these lines: It's a good promise God has given. If He delights in us He'll bring us into the fullness of that promise. He is with us. We must not fear.

The Anvil of Service

Joshua is described as the servant of Moses in Exodus 33:11 and Numbers 11:28 (KJV). This word 'servant' is an interesting word. The Hebrew word is 'sharath,' and it means to serve as a menial person or it means a worshiper. We can know outright that Joshua was not a worshiper of Moses, so let's look at this issue of serving as a menial person.

A 'sharath' is not a scullery maid or someone forced to work or someone "worked," if you will, as an animal would be worked. The word is always used in reference to a servant of higher rank — Joseph, for example, as he served in Potiphar's household or Abishag as he waited upon David. Even so, the word retains the implication of service as a menial person, a servile person, one who is humbly yielding or submissive. There is an implication of physical labor in which someone else is making the decisions — *all* the decisions.

Service as a 'sharath' is a good instrument for the forging of leaders; however, it is not a condition that comes easily to the nature of a gifted leader. At least three characteristics invaluable in leaders can be effectively acquired in 'sharath'-type service.

Restraint is the first. Restraint can be defined as an influence, action or instrument that restrains. Restraint speaks of a limitation or loss of liberty or of confinement. It speaks of the control of one's emotions, impulses and so on.

The capacity to control one's emotions and impulses as a benefit in our walk with God is immediately obvious. After all, Moses lost his place in the land God had given Israel because of a moment in which he was without restraint, in which he lost control of his emotions and impulses. In his loss of control he failed to rightly represent God to the people under his leadership. The people of Israel, a leader nation in God's design, experienced a 40-year 'hold' on the promise of God because they lost control of their emotions and impulses when confronted with walled cities and big giants.

To know and honor restraint, internal or external, whether by influence, action or instrument, is an essential component to the business of laying hold of the purpose and promise of God.

I think of a great rush or flood of water denied the liberty of — that is to say, restrained from — running unchecked across some bit of topography, confined instead to the inside of a strategically constructed pipeline. The pipeline which confines the water also concentrates the power of the water, directs the flow of the water to specific outlets and so gives to the water the force and focus of specific purpose.

This is a good thing for the water. It's a good thing for the purposes to which the water is directed. If you will hear it, the water becomes the 'sharath' of the one who picks the particular pipeline by which the water is confined. The water makes no decisions about its direction or its purpose. It only follows the path of the one who has chosen the pipeline.

Similarly a harness makes a 'sharath' out of a horse. The harness, with its attendant reins in the hands of a master, concentrates and focuses the strength of the horse in a given direction, which is not chosen by the horse. While the horse in its immaturity may chafe at the limitation of liberty that comes with the harness, the value of the horse in its maturity will have been exponentially increased by the early discipline of the harness. The horse becomes the 'sharath' of the one who selects the harness and the one who holds the reins.

Leaders in their immaturity are horsy. All leaders exhibit immaturity at points of time and/or in places of character. The value of the leader in maturity is exponentially increased by the discipline of the harness at points of time and places of character marked by immaturity.

A particular kind of restraint and the second characteristic that can be developed as one yields to the position of 'sharath' is the discipline of the tongue. The plain truth is we talk too much. Leaders are especially guilty of talking too much.

May I cite the Book of Ecclesiastes, chapter five, verse one: "Walk prudently when you go to the house of God; and draw near to hear rather than to give the sacrifice of fools..."

May I cite the Book of Proverbs, chapter 10, verse 19: "In the multitude of words sin is not lacking, but he who restrains his lips is wise."

When somebody else is calling the shots we learn to control our tongues. That principle needs no explanation. Those who have served another as a "menial person" understand completely.

Those who have not served another as a "menial person" will do so somewhere, sometime, and understanding will come.

The Lord is looking for people who can carry His heart, who can carry the secrets of His heart. He is looking for people who, as fellow workers with Him, can carry the weightier matters of His counsel. He is looking for people to whom He can speak and then say, "Shhhh! Don't tell anyone." And they won't tell anyone. If we want to be privy to the counsel of the Lord, we must learn to control our tongues. The 'sharath' will learn the skill.

Thirdly, service as a 'sharath' affords opportunity to learn how to quiet one's "soul even as a weaned child" (Psalm 131). The 'sharath' who serves in altogether unpleasant circumstances has opportunity to learn the quietness of soul that comes of knowing — really knowing — that his God is indeed sovereign over all and in all and beyond all and in spite of all.

The Anvil of Mentors and Teachers

I like Paul's words recorded in I Thessalonians 2:7-8: "...we were gentle among you, just as a nursing mother cherishes her own children. So, affectionately longing for you, we were well pleased to impart to you not only the Gospel of God, but also our own lives because you had become dear to us."

In matters divine, learning from mentors and teachers is not so much the acquisition of information as it is the importation of the excellency of another's life. William Shakespeare put these words in the mouth of his Julius Caesar: "For mine own part, I shall be glad to learn of noble men."

Ignoble men can transmit knowledge and information. Where the learning is importation of excellency and not transmission of information, we must choose carefully those from whom we learn. To be noble is to be elevated above everything that can dishonor reputation. It is to be free and to be generous. To be noble by definition is to be of excellent disposition and ready to receive truth.

One who is ready to receive truth is generous and free in exporting excellency because he knows the principles of God:

- "Freely you have received, freely give" (Matthew 10:8).

- "...He who sows sparingly will reap also sparingly, and he who sows bountifully will also reap bountifully" (II Corinthians 9:6).

- "...Whatever a man sows, that he will also reap" (Galatians 6:7).

A noble man will freely give of his excellency, knowing he will be increased by doing so. It is important that we choose noble men as mentors and teachers, and I count noble women as well as men, of course.

It is not always so that we can choose those in positions of authority over us, but we always can choose those from whom we import character, values, understanding of God's way and understanding of His nature. Noble men and women will give you leave to import into your life noble things from their own lives. Noble men and women will train us to noble things, even as Joshua was trained to noble things. What things? I will name three. There are others.

First and most critically, Joshua was trained to the presence of God. In Exodus 24:13 it is recorded that Joshua followed Moses up the mountain of God. Somewhere along the way and probably at Moses' direction, Joshua must have found himself a nice place to sit, while Moses went a little farther up, to speak face-to-face with God. There Joshua waited for 40 days and nights, and for 40 days and nights he was learning this: When God calls you into His presence you stay until He's ready for you to go.

I am particularly fond of a certain verse of Scripture that speaks of Joshua, Exodus 33:11:

"So the Lord spoke to Moses face to face, as a man speaks to his friend. And he (Moses) would return to the camp, but his servant Joshua, the son of Nun, a young man, did not depart from the tabernacle."

Now, I've read the commentaries that explain Joshua's remaining behind. He was, they say, left in charge of the tabernacle and so simply fulfilling his duty to care for the place of meeting. That's reasonable, sort of. Another commentary says that Moses left Joshua there because it was not fitting for the tabernacle to be empty while God was present. It's difficult for me to picture Moses leaving the presence of God before God had finished His business.

I see something more. For whatever kind of practical reason Moses might have had in leaving Joshua at the tabernacle, I see Joshua pursuing God for the kind of excellency he had witnessed in the relationship between God and Moses. I like to think that Joshua, having an opportunity to stay behind, alone, in the presence of God, seized the opportunity that was before him. I see Joshua figuring it out: "If Moses' face can shine from the presence of God, maybe mine can, too, if I can get in God's presence the way Moses does. If Moses can hear God talk, maybe I can hear God talk, too, if I can just find out what it is He wants to talk about."

As Moses' 'sharath,' Joshua more than anyone else had opportunity to witness first-hand the dynamic of the presence of God in the life of Moses. I like to think that Joshua saw in that dynamic something he wanted; that Moses, just by being Moses, stirred in Joshua a hunger that pressed him beyond the simple, practical business of being trained as Moses' assistant. This is the kind of hunger, by the way, that determines whether one has faith and energy to build or whether one is willing only to gather what is left lying around; whether one is willing to content himself with whatever falls at his feet and can be picked up without strain or whether one is willing to dig the copper out of the hills (Deuteronomy 8:9).

Joshua was a man who would have dug copper out of the hills with his bare hands if that had become necessary. He had set himself to know this God Who spoke to Moses and to Whom Moses spoke, and he went into the import business with gusto. He brought into his own life everything that could be brought into his life from his daily contact with Moses. And we can know that Moses, being a noble man, would have been glad for him to do so.

First and most critically, Joshua was trained to the presence of God.

Secondly, Joshua was trained to discernment. On his way down the mountain from one of those journeys with Moses, Joshua heard a hue and cry from the camp. Moses heard it, too.

As a young man, Joshua said to his mentor, "There is a noise of war in the camp" (Exodus 32:17).

Moses, a much older man, corrected Joshua's hearing. "It is not the voice of those who shout in victory, nor is it the voice of those who cry out in defeat, but the voice of those who sing that I hear" (Exodus 32:18).

"No, Joshua," Moses said. "We're not hearing a battle going on. We're hearing a party." Moses was training Joshua to hear, to listen carefully, to discern, to make distinctions and not to make assumptions. We hear the echo of these lessons as Joshua, face-to-face with the Captain of the Lord's Hosts, refuses to assume friend or foe, but rather sets about to make the distinction: Whose side are You on, anyway?

Joshua was trained to discernment.

Thirdly, Joshua was trained to make choices. Leaders make choices all the time.

When leaders build teams they make choices — which people will work together and which ones won't and which ones need to work together so they'll have to get along with somebody they don't like. When leaders assign responsibility they make choices — who is suited to this task and who is suited to that one. When leaders distribute rewards and promotions, they make choices — which persons are deserving of reward and which persons are not, and who are the ones that just need to be surprised and encouraged by some reward undeserved.

Moses trained Joshua to make choices. When it came time to engage Amalek in battle, Moses himself could have picked the warriors and assigned them to Joshua. Instead, he let Joshua pick, and, in fighting alongside the men he'd chosen, Joshua was able to discover for himself where his choices had been good and where, not so good.

Joshua was trained to make good choices. The training served him well at the edge of a promise, where he chose to believe God, in spite of the giants, in spite of the walled cities.

The Anvil of the Word of God

Psalm 105:17-19: "He (God) sent a man before them — Joseph, who was sold as a slave. They hurt his feet with fetters; he was laid in irons. Until the time that His (God's) word came to pass, the word of the Lord tested him."

It could as well be said: "The word of the Lord proved him." When God proves us it is always, my pastor says, to show us approved.

We should know by the evidence of creation that God is a God of process. The Creator could have created everything complete and fully mature. He chose to create by process. The six-day process of creation produced a world that functions, multiplies and renews itself in process. Seedtime and harvest is process. Reproduction in animals, insects, birds and humans is process. The coming of the word of the Lord to us is seedtime and harvest. It is process. The word comes as a seed and begins to produce in us, what God has spoken to us, thus proving that we are who God has said we are. Joseph had a dream; actually, two dreams (Genesis 37). In the first he and his family were binding sheaves in a field. Suddenly, Joseph's sheaf rose and stood upright, while everybody else's sheaves stood all around and bowed to the ground. In the second dream the sun, moon and eleven stars bowed down to Joseph. Nobody besides God and Joseph liked either of those dreams. In fact, at least 10 of the eleven "stars" got downright hostile about them, and the sun, i.e., Joseph's father, rebuked his favorite son.

"What is this dream that you have dreamed? Shall your mother and I and your brothers indeed come to bow down to the earth before you?"

And there began a long and potentially confusing process by which the word of the Lord that had come to Joseph began to prove that Joseph was who God had said he was. At the end of that process, between chapters 42 and 49 of Genesis, it is recorded at least four times that Joseph's brothers fell down or bowed themselves before Him. Apart from that very literal bowing down, Joseph's father and brothers lived in Egypt under Joseph's rule, a governmental bowing down.

In another instance, David was anointed king over Israel by the prophet of God, and there began a long and potentially confusing process by which the word of the Lord that had come to David began to prove that David was, indeed, king over Israel, just as God had said.

The coming of the word of the Lord begins a seedtime and harvest process. In the space of time between the deposit of the seed and its maturity, the seed itself, the word of the Lord, tests us to prove that we are who God has said we are.

The word of the Lord came to Joshua: With Caleb, Joshua will go into the land.

For 40 years the word of the Lord tested Joshua, to show him approved. The word of the Lord will test us, as well, to show us approved.

It's part of what makes Joseph a Joseph, David a David and Joshua a Joshua.

The Anvil of the Sovereign Works of the Holy Spirit, Personalized

Personal moments with God:

"So the Lord spoke to Moses face to face, as a man speaks to his friend. And he would return to the camp, but his servant Joshua the son of Nun, a young man, did not depart from the tabernacle" (Exodus 33:11).

"'What is this dream that you have dreamed? Shall your mother and I and your brothers indeed come to bow down to the earth before you?' And his brothers envied him, but his father kept the matter in mind"(Genesis 37:10-11).

"...Joseph and (Jesus') mother marveled at those things which were spoken of Him" (Luke 2:33).

"...Mary kept all these things and pondered them in her heart" (Luke 2:19).

"And the Child grew and became strong in spirit, filled with wisdom; and the grace of God was upon Him" (Luke 2:40).

God has revealed Himself with liberality. He has been generous to give glimpses of many moments, great and ordinary, between Himself and those He loves. As liberal as He has been, as generous, He has been jealous, as well, over so many of the intimate places in His interaction with Jesus and with the men and women whose lives are recorded in Scripture. We would like to know: What happened between Joshua and God after Moses left the tabernacle? What did the Lord say to Joseph in the quiet place of his heart as he thought on the words spoken over the infant Jesus? What did the Spirit of God say to Mary as she pondered? What did He do in Jacob's life as the patriarch thought on Joseph's dreams and observed his sons?

There are vast numbers of unrecorded moments in which the Father has embraced, in which the Holy Spirit has brooded over, in which the Word has whispered tenderly to the heart and soul of a king or priest or prophet or warrior or barren woman. We don't know what was said, what intimate working was underway. The sovereign God is sovereignly discreet. There is a marrow in His relationship with you, in His relationship with me that no one outside of that relationship can know. If we were to attempt to speak of it, they still would not know, for it cannot be shared. Beyond all, these are the places in which Joshuas are made. We must find these places for ourselves.

One More Thought…

Joshua was mentored. Joshua was taught. Joshua also taught himself. He taught himself to stay where God was. Whether it was 40 days on the mountain, waiting for Moses to finish his conversation with the Lord, or whether it was 40 years in the wilderness, waiting for an unbelieving generation to die off, Joshua stayed where God was.

How many people walk away from a vision because the wait is too long? How many people quit waiting because too many years have passed? What has been lost to the Kingdom of God because we have not quieted our souls to stay where God is until He finishes what He started? He always finishes what He starts, you know.

We must train ourselves to stay where God is. It begins in

small things. When the alarm clock goes off in the morning, where is God? Where are you? When a relationship becomes torn and twisted and the pain of it seems unbearable, where is God? And where are you? When faith seems foolish and unbelief holds out seemingly great advantage, where is God? Where are you? When God is slandered, where are you?

If we are to be people of faith, if we are to be people of vision, if we are to be healed of disappointment — and the body of Christ desperately needs to be healed of disappointment — then we must, in small matters and great, find out where God is and get there and stay there. (Luke 9:10-17, 46-48, 51-56; Acts 16:5-10; II Corinthians 2:10.)

When the Son of Man comes, shall He find faith? These words are not for the "end times." These words are for today. These words are for you and these words are for me. When God shows up in our waiting, where will we be? At the end of the Book of Deuteronomy, Israel is camped once again only a river away from the promise of God. Forty years of death and wilderness are behind them. An uncrossable river is in front of them. And nothing is moving. Nothing.

Yet, the promise is only three days away.

Chapter 9

Tonic from the Most High

"He heals those who are broken in heart:
and gives medicine to heal their sickness."
Psalm 147:3

A word about God's "suddenlies." We've said it before. God's "suddenlies" are not. They look like "suddenlies." They seem to happen all at once. If you're someone who has a talent for seeing only the moment at hand, you'll call it a "suddenly." However, God's "suddenlies" are anything but.

Suddenly means hastily. I suppose that in the economy of God's throne room, eternity being all that it is, anything and everything that occurs in this scrunched up thing called time and space seems to occur hastily. However, if time and space is the thing in which you've stretched yourself out and you're counting minutes, hours, days, weeks, months, years and maybe decades, then 'hasty' is not a word you would ascribe to the activity of God. Hasty is precipitous. To be precipitous is to hurry blindly or rashly, is to proceed without due deliberation. Not God's way. Not His way at all.

Suddenly means without preparation. When God has a plan He gives us all the preparation we will allow Him to give us, all that we will receive, all that we need. When God has a plan He prepares the historical context, the geographic context and the hearts of the people. He sets the stage and He does it well, as He does everything well. God's "suddenlies" are not sudden.

It could be said that Sarah was "suddenly" pregnant with Isaac, and, indeed, the actual moment of conception was just that, a mere moment. But the so-called "suddenly" was 25 years in the making. It began on record when Abraham was 75 years old, and God said, among other things, "I will make you a great nation" (Genesis 12:2).

Later, God amplified: "...He that shall come forth out of your own bowels will be your heir" (Genesis 15:4).

Still later, "Sarah, your wife, shall have a son" (Genesis 18:10). When Abraham was 100 years old, the son showed up. The seed of the nation came to be, and the nation itself began to be born.

It could be said that Jesus was "suddenly" conceived of the Holy Ghost in the womb of a young lady named Mary. The conception happened in the wink of an eye, it's true, but the plan was in the eternal hopper before the foundation of the world (Revelation 13:8b). Israel, which was to receive the Messiah, was prepared with a generous slathering of prophetic pronouncement as to the nature of Jesus' time, coming, purpose and ministry.

It could be said that Israel "suddenly" stepped to the edge of the Jordan, then crossed the river into the land God had promised Abraham, Isaac and Jacob, but that's exactly the point. The land had been promised to Abraham, Isaac and Jacob. The "suddenly" was many generations and a very long time in coming.

The Book of Deuteronomy ends and the Book of Joshua begins in a so-near-yet-so-far place. So near: God's people are camped right at the edge of promise. So far: Nothing is moving forward. Then, "suddenly," as it would seem, it's time not to be at the edge but to go in.

"Suddenly," as it would seem, things that have not moved at all begin moving very quickly. This is what the jarring from God is all about. The whack against the table edge jolts us out of our "stuck-on-hold" places wherever they may be found in our spirits, souls and bodies. The sudden whack puts us in a place to move — internally and externally — so that we can begin to discover what the wilderness has done to us and for us that makes us ready to go in.

The Book of Joshua opens with all the pieces in place. Indeed, the wilderness has done its work. A rebellious and unbelieving generation has passed from the scene. A new generation, one able to enter and possess, has come to maturity. The people are in place, and so is the leader who will lead the people out of disappointment into appointment. In the opening chapters of the Book, God is just about ready to administer to His hope-sick people the appropriate cure:

"Hope deferred makes the heart sick; but when the desire comes it is a tree of life."

The desire is about to come. God's people are about to eat from this particular "tree of life." The cure is on the way. But before the cure appropriate to the condition is administered, there is instruction to be given, actually two sets of instructions, one set for the leader, one set for the people. By looking closely at these instructions, we can identify elements — ingredients, we'll call them — of a pre-curative medication. This concept of pre-curative medication will not be foreign to us if we have even the slightest familiarity with procedures common to the practice of physical medicine. It frequently happens that a sick person is not strong enough to endure the cure for his condition (another book, entirely), and so the prescribed undertaking is delayed until pre-curative medication has added to the patient strength enough to benefit from medical procedures. How many surgeries are delayed until the patient is strong enough to survive the surgery?

God's cures often come under the heading of "suddenlies." It would seem as if they happen suddenly, and if we are more tuned in to the moment at hand than we are to the history of a matter, we would marvel at the "suddenly-ness" of what God has done. However, as is true of most "suddenlies," so it is true of God's cures — they don't happen suddenly. Most cures — not all, but most — are preceded by the daily administration of a tonic over a long period of time. Let's look at this word 'tonic.'

Tonic…literal meaning, increasing tension. "Tonic power" is amplified strength derived from increased tension. In the field of medicine a tonic is that which increases the strength or tone of an anatomical or organic system. It's something that opposes and removes the effects of debility — debility being, in this case, the impact of a hope-sick heart. Tonic is something that restores healthy function. A tonic is a medicine that increases the tone of the muscular fiber and gives vigor and action to the system.

When dreams have been delayed and vision has been postponed, when the cry of the heart has been on hold for a long time, it is very often true that before "the desire comes" God begins daily administration of a tonic to increase strength, to add "tonic power," to tone the system, to oppose and remove the effects of delay-induced debility and to restore the system to healthy function. When the desire shows up, the effects of the pre-curative tonic enable us to survive the shock of change from delay to realization and to seize the promise of God in a healthy, promise-sustaining way.

And so the children of Israel, camped by the Jordan, stand in need of a tonic. Much of the tonic necessary to the season has been administered already. A little more of it comes in these last days, the days between the wilderness and the fulfillment of hope. Let's take a look at the tonic of God.

For the Leader

It's not uncommon for the Scriptures to speak of oil in relationship to healing. Scripture notes that the proper direction for the flow of oil is from the head to the skirts of the garment, top to bottom (Psalm 133). It's reasonable to conclude that the same direction of flow would be good also for a flow of tonic, so the tonic would have come first to Joshua. Because God gives exactly what is needed in every situation, to every person, we can know what Joshua needed by what God gave. God first gave a fresh charge out of His own mouth.

Joshua 1:1-2: "After the death of Moses the servant of the Lord, it came to pass that the Lord spoke to Joshua the son of Nun, Moses' assistant, saying: 'Moses My servant is dead.'"

Bone-jarring words for a disappointed people. The Lord spoke to Joshua — to Joshua himself, personally, one-to-one: "Moses is dead." God had buried the body of Moses and God didn't tell anybody where the body was. See it from Joshua's point of view. Moses had stayed on mountains for a long time on numbers of occasions. How was Joshua to know whether Moses was dead or whether he would be back in a jiffy? He had only the words of God's mouth to tell him what was what.

More of verse 2: "Now therefore, arise, go over this Jordan, you and all this people, to the land which I am giving to them..."

Past is past. Future is future. "It's time, Joshua," God was saying, "for you to take leadership of this group of people." How was Joshua to know it was his turn at bat? He knew it was time because God said so. The issue is always: Did God say so?

Verse 6: "Be strong and of good courage, for to this people you shall divide as an inheritance the land which I swore to their fathers to give them."

There is the order: Take the people into the land; apportion the land to the people.

Why would Joshua need a new charge from God's mouth? He'd been trained and nurtured in his knowledge of God by Moses. He'd been hand-picked by God to lead the people into the land — Moses would have told him so. He'd been brought before the high priest and all the congregation, in the sight of whom Moses had laid hands on Joshua and given him charge. Why, who else would lead besides Joshua?! And he already had his charge. Yet, he needed a new one. Why?

Consider and remember: In the beginning the issue was the words of God's mouth. Now that Moses is dead and new leadership is needed, the issue is still the words of God's mouth.

It's been a long walk — 40 years long. Joshua has been a perseverer extraordinaire, a hanger-in-there par excellence. Sometimes perseverers exraordinaire and hangers-in-there par excellence get to wondering: Is this thing in which I'm persevering, is this thing I'm "hangin' in there with," is it still God? It started with God. Is He still giving it the gas that's making it go, or did He, somewhere along the way, abandon this plan and go on to something else? Did I miss the signal? Am I stubbornly clinging to a stale plan, trying to pick fruit out of season? Or is this thing still in God's heart? If He were to speak today, would He speak the same thing He spoke at the beginning?"

We live by the words that continually proceed from God's

mouth, not the words that came from His mouth five years ago. Or the words that might come from His mouth 10 years from now. We live by the words that continually proceed from His mouth, the 'today' words. The words that came from His mouth five years ago need to be heard in 'today' words, not because God's words get old, but because we need the tonic of the word that is alive today.

When we are leading people out of a long season of disappointment and delay, we need 'today' words from God's mouth to initiate forward motion. The words of the Lord are eternal and ever-living, but the organic "system," you and me, in which those promises have lain dormant, needs to be invigorated. It needs to be toned and strengthened by the freshness of the spoken word, lest we find ourselves moving in the presumption of habit.

For a number of years I've carried in my heart a specific spoken instruction from God. During this period of time, and on several occasions there have been opportunities, presumably from God, that would have seemed to indicate a change of direction. On each of these occasions, I've gone to the Lord and asked, "Lord, is the original instruction still good? Are You altering my course, or do I just not see how this opportunity fits with the original instruction?"

Each time, to avoid moving by habit, I've required from God some indication, verbal or otherwise: "Should I continue to carry this instruction and move in accordance with it? Is this opportunity from You, or is it distraction or diversion?"

We live by the words of His mouth — the continually proceeding words from His mouth — not by force of habit. Every leader needs to lead in the freshness of the words from God's mouth, not from habit. Certainly Joshua was no exception.

Consider also:

Joshua was not going into the land as Moses' servant, Caleb's peer, one of 12 spies or just another traveler in a 40-year wilderness walk. Joshua was no longer in the official position of servant to the chief. He was no longer a peer to Caleb. It had been a long time since he'd been one of the 12 spies and he'd never walked that 40-year wilderness walk as just another traveler. He was always, at the very least, one of only two of the adults that came out of Egypt, who would set foot down in the promise of God.

Joshua's earlier charge to lead the people into the land had come to him as to a leader-in-training. Now he stands at the head of a nation, the "father" of a nation, so to speak. Now the decisions are his to make and his to be responsible for under God.

Someone whose view I respect once told me, "The king sees things differently than those who are not king. That's why the king is the king."

However truly Joshua-the-servant-to-Moses saw the position and the place and the task that belonged to Israel, Joshua-the-leader-of-the-nation saw it even more clearly, even more fully, even more accurately.

Has God made you a warrior and is your preparation underway? You see very clearly, now, what the battlefield looks like and how the battle must be won. Hear this: No matter how clearly you see now, when you stand on the field, with your sword drawn, you will see even more clearly than you do now.

Has God made you a "king," a ruler of some sort or another, and is your preparation underway? Is it very plain to you now, how you are to function in your sphere of authority and what decisions must be made in order for the hand of God to be free to work? If it's very plain to you now, it will be oh-so-much plainer when you stand in the mantle God has designed for you. You will see differently then, more fully, more accurately. That's why the ruler is the ruler.

It was necessary for Joshua that a fresh charge from God come to him in his place as leader of the nation. His eyes were different in that place. His ears were different. And even if God had spoken the precise words He'd spoken before, without the slightest alteration, the words would have come differently into the heart of Joshua and, therefore, differently into the heart of the nation.

Joshua had need of something else. He needed a fresh charge from God, yes, but he also needed a reiteration of the charge spoken many years before.

"Every place that the sole of your foot will tread upon I have given you, as I said to Moses. From the wilderness and this Lebanon as far as the great river, the River Euphrates, all the land of the Hittites, and to the Great Sea toward the going down of the sun, shall be your territory" (Joshua 1:3-4).

The boundaries had been laid down for Abraham (Genesis 15:18-21) and surely carried through the generations in the stories told by the fathers to the children. Joshua and the people he led needed to know that the wilderness had not changed their destiny. The land was still theirs. The losses of the wilderness — and they were massive — hadn't altered the destiny. Instead of altering the destiny, the waiting time, with all the losses and all the new things birthed, had shaped and formed a people able to take hold of that destiny.

The wilderness doesn't alter our destiny. It puts us on a collision course with our destiny. This is good to remember when the wilderness nights get long and cold. The losses and the births are spelling out your destiny.

Too, Joshua needed confidence that God was for him and not from a distance. Verses 5 and 9: "No man shall be able to stand before you all the days of your life; as I was with Moses, so I will be with you. I will not leave you or forsake you....Be strong and of good courage; do not be afraid, nor be dismayed, for the Lord your God is with you wherever you go."

It wasn't enough that God was with Israel coming out of Egypt 40-plus years ago or crossing the Red Sea or in the battle with the Amalekites or in the manna. It wasn't good enough that God was with Moses. Joshua had to know that God was with him personally. He had to know that this God was not a distant God, that He was an up-close God. He had been an up-close God with Moses. Joshua needed an up-close God, too.

I need an up-close God. Recently, on two occasions, I have awakened in the middle of a night, aware of a distinct presence both in the room and filling the room. It was the "keeping presence" of God. Now, I can't explain how I knew it was, in particular, His "keeping presence," but I knew it. The up-close God was keeping me, and He wanted me to know it. I need this kind of God, and so do you. Especially do we need this kind of God when our disappointed feet are about to take a few new steps into a land that has caused us pain in previous seasons, even as Israel's feet were standing in a place where there was a history of pain. Joshua needed confidence. God was willing to supply.

Let's do a second take on verse 5 and add to it this time verse 6: "No man shall be able to stand before you all the days of your life; as I was with Moses, so I will be with you. I will not leave you nor forsake you. Be strong and of good courage, for to this people you shall divide as an inheritance the land which I swore to their fathers to give them."

It is necessary with God to read between the lines. Even between the words. God can make Himself heard plainly and He does that, but more often there are nuances and implications hidden, tucked away in what God says and we must listen carefully and listen deeply to understand.

Hear, please: "...you shall divide as an inheritance the land which I swore to their fathers to give them."

In these words is the assurance for Joshua that the march into the land of Canaan will be successful. No matter what battles will have to be fought, no matter what in-camp issues will have to be resolved, no matter what discoveries Israel will make about cities and people or about themselves and their readiness or lack of readiness to possess what God had promised — no matter what — Joshua will distribute among the children of Israel the land God "swore to their fathers to give them."

Hear a little more deeply: In this assurance of success is the announcement that this entry into destiny will not be "a piece of cake." With God's promise of success is the implication that there will be opportunity for failure. With His promise of victory is the implication that there will be opportunity for defeat. God is letting Joshua know: This land has been given; you will have to win it.

I appreciate that God doesn't allow us to be ambushed. He gives hints. He gives clues, and if we are alert to His manner of speaking, we will not be caught off-guard or unduly surprised by opposition that comes our way. We may not always know the exact nature of the opposition that's coming, but we will be alert to the fact the opposition in some form or fashion is on the way.

It was a clear, sunshine-filled, warm-but-not-too-warm day in the fall some years ago when I sat down to breakfast with a thick, hot, well-buttered slice of banana-nut bread in my hand. I opened my mouth wide to receive that early morning treat. At the very moment my mouth opened, with the banana-nut bread only an inch away from my teeth, God said, "No weapon formed against you shall prosper" (Isaiah 54:17).

I lost my appetite for banana-nut bread. If God felt it necessary to assure me at the moment that no weapon formed against me would prosper, then it must be that somewhere out there, beyond my breakfast table, outside my front door, perhaps, there was a weapon formed against me. My conclusion: This would not be the best moment to indulge myself with banana-nut bread. Better to fast.

To be ambushed is to be suddenly attacked from a concealed situation. Ambushes can result in grievous casualty counts and loss of ground. God specializes in "un-concealing" concealed situations, thus foiling ambushes.

Joshua needed more than simple assurance that the advance into Canaan would be successful; he needed a "heads-up" in regard to the road that lay ahead. God, the best provider, made provision.

Finally, let me list four things Joshua needed to lead the people out and in — out of disappointment and into stewardship of the promise of God. They can be found in the first chapter of the Book of Joshua, verses 7-9 and 16-18.

The words of God to Joshua, verses 7-9:

"Only be strong and very courageous, that you may observe to do according to all the law which Moses My servant commanded you; do not turn from it to the right hand or to the left, that you may prosper wherever you go. This Book of the Law shall not depart from your mouth, but you shall meditate in it day and night, that you may observe to do according to all that is written in it. For then you will make your way prosperous, and then you will have good success. Have not I commanded you? Be strong and of good courage; do not be afraid, nor be dismayed, for the Lord your God is with you wherever you go."

Words from the people to Joshua, verses 16-18:

"All that you command us we will do, and wherever you send

us we will go. Just as we heeded Moses in all things, so we will heed you. Only the Lord your God be with you, as He was with Moses. Whoever rebels against your command and does not heed your words, in all that you command him, shall be put to death. Only be strong and of good courage."

First, Joshua needed a radical obedience: "Observe to do according to all the law which Moses My servant commanded you..."

Secondly, Joshua needed an awareness of the consequences of disobedience. A reminder of those consequences came through the mouths of the people, in the words recorded in verse 18: "Whoever rebels against your command and does not heed your words, in all that you command him, shall be put to death."

The words were spoken by the people about the people, but it would have been easy for Joshua to figure it out: If it's so very critical for the people to obey the commands issued by the human leader, how much more critical is it for the human leader to obey the commands of God. All along the trail through the wilderness there were graves bearing witness to the consequences of disobedience.

Radical obedience is greatly facilitated by keen awareness of the consequences of disobedience. Radical: Again, to the root, something that is part of our essence, part of who we are. It's obedience that comes without second thought. This kind of obedience is not acquired in an instant. It's the fruit of a lifetime in which the words of God's mouth have become the words of my mouth by way of my heart. That's a good thing to remember: The words of God's mouth become the words of my mouth by way of my heart.

This kind of obedience is most evident in ready response to what is, in its nature, an impossible command. Example: Joshua is commanded to, "Be strong...Be courageous...Be of good courage...Do not be afraid...Do not be dismayed."

These words — afraid, dismayed — are "feeling" words. They describe feelings that get in the way of my being strong and courageous. I don't know about your feelings, but my feelings are quite rambunctious and willful and tend to rise and fall without rhyme or reason. How can I hope to corral such things as my feelings in order to obey such a command?

Joshua didn't concern himself with whatever feelings he may have had about the impossibility of the command. He simply busied himself doing the things that people do when they're strong and courageous and not afraid and not dismayed. He commanded his officers, gave charge to his people and set up a team of men to view the land again.

My pastor puts it this way: "Whatever you would do if you were not afraid, do that."

This kind of obedience is greatly assisted by radical focus, and that's the third thing Joshua needed.

"...Do not turn from (the command) to the right hand or to the left...this Book of the Law shall not depart from your mouth... you shall meditate in it day and night..."

Radical focus. Day and night means no time available for worrying about giants and walled cities and grasshoppers. Day and night means all the time. All the time means God's commands are carried in our hearts and minds 24-hours-a-day, seven-days-a-week. Sometimes they're on the front burner, sometimes on the back, but they're always present. Our ears are continually inclined to the words God has spoken to us and by which we live. We are continually aligning, realigning and adjusting our thoughts, activities, attitudes, plans and strategies in accordance with God's written directives and His spoken instructions. This kind of day-and-night focus is radical and necessary in moments when possessing promise is at the top of the agenda.

May I interject something important here? It will be good to remember this:

- Strength will not possess without courage.

- Strength and courage will not possess without radical obedience.

- Strength and courage and radical obedience will not possess without radical focus.

Remember Samson. Remember Saul. Remember Lot's wife. Remember Lot. Remember Peter in his worst moments and in his best, and then hear it again: Strength will not possess without courage — Strength and courage will not possess without radical obedience — Strength and courage and radical obedience will not possess without radical focus.

The fourth essential ingredient in the tonic for Joshua: He would need to know that when he got where he was going, the nation of which he was the leader would be standing there behind him. That confidence came from the pledge of the people.

"All that you command us we'll do," the people said. "Wherever you send us we'll go."

Let me tell you about an experience of leadership that belongs to a lady whom we'll call Suzanne. Suzanne was the appointed leader of a team of six tambourinists, scheduled to play on a particular evening in her home church. There were many experienced tambourinists in her church, each one of them a skillful team player. It so happened that on this particular evening none of the experienced tambourinists were on her team, only the beginners.

Suzanne knew the first rule of the tambourine team: Follow the leader. Whatever the leader does, all the people on the team do it, too, even if it's wrong. After all, if you're banging wrong on six tambourines, it's best if everyone is banging wrong together. The beginners knew the rule, but during the evening it became very apparent that knowing the rule and proceeding according to the rule are two different things, especially for beginners.

At some point during the worship service, Suzanne felt a strong leading from God to climb the steps to the platform where the preacher and the musicians were holding forth. Now, this is an unusual move, but would not have been unduly startling under normal tambourine circumstances, and so Suzanne, experienced and confident, took off, fully expecting that her team was close behind. She marched boldly. She marched with her head held high. She pounded her tambourine in a most militant way. As she approached the preacher, who happened to be leading worship, Suzanne turned to the congregation, only to discover that the congregation included the other five members of her team, frozen in their spots on the main floor of the sanctuary and staring at their leader — the only tambourinist on the platform — "like calves at a new gate," as Suzanne herself expressed it.

Suzanne never missed a beat. She made a quick turn, marched herself across the platform and down the steps and joined her followers and the rest of the congregation. What is it they say? "I'm their leader — which way did they go?"

It would have been encouraging for Suzanne had her followers followed her to the platform. So with Joshua, He needed to know that his followers would follow. He needed to know that when he arrived on the other side of the Jordan, he wouldn't be standing there alone.

For the People

Just as Joshua's God-muscles needed to be strengthened and toned, so those same kinds of muscles in the people needed to be strengthened and toned. In fact, some of the pre-curative tonic administered to the leader splashed on the people without change of ingredients.

As Joshua was in need both of a fresh charge and of a reiteration of the earlier charge, so were the people. The new and the old came in one fell swoop.

Verses 10 and 11 of Joshua chapter one:

"Then Joshua commanded the officers of the people, saying, 'Pass through the camp and command the people (to) prepare provisions for (themselves), for within three days (we) will cross over this Jordan, to go in to possess the land which the Lord (our) God is giving (us) to possess...Remember the word which Moses the servant of the Lord commanded you, saying, The Lord your God is giving you rest and is giving you this land."

The original charge was reiterated: There is still a river to cross. There is still a possessing that must occur. The land is the same. The wilderness hasn't changed your destiny. The Lord is giving you exactly what He promised.

But that reiterated charge came with freshness: Within three days you're going in!

Imagine the excitement! Forty years of waiting, 40 years of dying, 40 years of wandering, and God says, "Within three days."

Some of you reading this need to hear that: Within three days! That for which you have waited, that for which you've been prepared, that for which you have hungered, that about which you have entertained the notion, "It cannot happen now — too many years, too much pain, too many opportunities lost."

Nevertheless — within three days.

Possession of the promise would demand of Joshua strength, courage, radical focus and radical obedience to the words of God. These same demands would be made on the people, with this added: For the nation of Israel, possession of God's promise would call for radical obedience to the words of God through the God-appointed leader, perhaps a more difficult demand to meet as it calls for trust not only in God but in the leader He has appointed. Hear again Israel's commitment to Joshua:

"All that you command us we will do, and wherever you send us we will go. Just as we heeded Moses in all things, so we will heed you. Only the Lord your God be with you, as He was with Moses. Whoever rebels against your command and does not heed your words, in all that you command him, shall be put to death. Only be strong and of good courage."

It seems excessively obvious to point out that this kind radical commitment is most readily given to a leader of strength. Leaders of strength are neither threatened by nor offended in those seasons designed by God to demonstrate that the confidence of the people is safe in his — or her — hands.

Strength in God is not a gift to anyone. Strength in God is built. In like manner, the deep-seated confidence of people is not a gift. It is built. As followers, we can choose to engage in external behaviors that express trust and confidence in a leader. In fact, more often than not, it will be necessary to begin a follower/leader relationship from a platform of external behaviors. However, subsequent to that very formal kind of beginning, the quality and nature of the leader's interaction with those in his care will have one of two effects on the followers: It will build in them trust that moves from the arena of external behavior to settle deeply into their spirits and souls, or it will erode whatever small measure of confidence enabled them to begin the relationship in the first place.

The confidence expressed by the nation of Israel toward Joshua was constructed during their history together. It was built day-to-day as the people came to know Joshua — and, it may be added, as Joshua came to know the people. Heart-confidence is laid into a relationship layer by layer by layer, and the laying in of this heart-confidence is essential to the relationship between a leader and a disappointed people about to become un-disappointed.

Disappointment is a wound in the soul. An appointment that should have been and wasn't, makes a wound in the soul — even when responsibility for the disappointment is my own, maybe especially when the responsibility is my own. Apart from heart-confidence in the one who leads, disappointed people will follow only at a safe distance. If a people is to possess the promise of God together, then that safe distance must be crossed over and closed up. On the part of followers, the external behavior of confidence in a leader — we'll call it simple obedience — makes a way for the safe distance to be crossed over and closed up. On the part of leaders, the absence of offense in the proving season stretches a long way across the cautious distance between himself — or herself — and the wounds of the disappointed.

Other ingredients in the tonic:

To possess together, or individually for that matter, there must be separation together (and/or individually) to the words of God's mouth. Joshua told the people, "Sanctify yourselves ... for tomorrow the Lord will do wonders among you" (Joshua 3:5).

Sanctify...consecrate...separate yourselves — not to the land, not to the leader, not to the other people who are with you — sanctify yourselves to the words of God's mouth.

"(For the Lord) humbled you, allowed you to hunger, and fed you with manna which you did not know nor did your fathers know, that He might make you know that man shall not live by bread alone; but man lives by every word that proceeds from the mouth of the Lord" (Deuteronomy 8:3).

Obedience to the words of a leader is an external matter and can be managed easily by the well-disciplined soul. Separation to the words of God's mouth is an internal matter. It's a heart issue. It's a condition of living that comes from the wellspring of a healthy spirit.

Separation to the words of God's mouth is something immeasurably greater than simple obedience, although simple obedience is very desirable in and of itself. Obedience responds to instruction and direction but may reserve for itself many matters of the heart that lie outside the immediate sphere of whatever instruction and direction may come.

Separation to the words of God's mouth is an internal condition in which everything, in every sphere of life, is given in advance to whatever words God may speak. And if the words God speaks give a different direction on a daily basis, then the life so given changes direction on a daily basis, giving no thought to and entertaining no concern about the direction abandoned.

Separation to the words of God's mouth is part and parcel of loving God with all our hearts, souls, minds and strength. Nothing is reserved for oneself, nothing held back. Every corner of the heart is open and yielded to the desires of God.

Obedience hears instruction and direction and commandments and acts accordingly. Separation to the words of God's mouth pursues the inclinations of God, seeks out His preferences, digs for the secrets in His heart and treasures every nugget so discovered. Separation to the words of God's mouth makes for radical commitment to obedience that goes beyond external behaviors, to the root, to the essence of who we are, and then springs up into life from that place. It is necessary equipment for those who would possess promise.

Also essential to the going-in: Another look at the land in question. In chapter two of the Book of Joshua, the Israelites revisit the spy-plan with a new twist — not 12 spies this time, only two. Joshua, remember, has streamlined the decision-making process. Not 24 eyes to see but only four. Not 24 ears to hear but only four. Not 12 mouths to speak but only two.

"Go, view the land, especially Jericho," Joshua told them.

Let's take a look at this thing again...from the other side of unbelief. Are the people really as strong as we were told? Let's look at those cities again. Are they as fortified as we were told? Are the walls as high, are the cities as big? Let's look again at the giants. Are they really as tall as we were told? And what about us? Do we look as grasshopper-ish as we did then? Let's get another report. It surely must have been that in the memory of a dying, unbelieving generation those giants got bigger and God's people smaller with every step they took in the opposite direction of God's best plan. The time had come for another look at the land.

Two spies work better than 12. Joshua Chapter Two, verses 23-24: "So the two men returned (from their spy duties)...and they came to Joshua the son of Nun, and told him all that had befallen them. And they said to Joshua, 'Truly the Lord has delivered all the land into our hands, for indeed all the inhabitants of the country are faint-hearted because of us.'"

Now, where did they get an idea like that? They got it from Rahab, a citizen of Jericho. It was Rahab who had said:

"I know that the Lord has given you the land, that the terror of you has fallen on us, and that all the inhabitants of the land are faint-hearted because of you. For we have heard how the Lord dried up the water of the Red Sea for you when you came out of Egypt, and what you did to the two kings of the Amorites who were on the other side of the Jordan, Sihon and Og, whom you utterly destroyed.And as soon as we heard these things, our hearts melted; neither did there remain any more courage in anyone because of you, for the Lord your God, He is God in heaven above and on earth beneath" (Joshua 2:9-11).

Did you hear it? "We heard how the Lord dried up the Red Sea," Rahab told the spies. "We heard what you did to the Amorites on the other side of the Jordan, and to Sihon and to Og. Our hearts melted. There was no courage."

Do you hear it? Except for unbelief, Israel could have had the land 40 years earlier. Not all instances of delayed vision come from unbelief, but for those of you who fit the picture, who've been to the edge and turned back, who've had your toes on the border of your destiny and run away, or been driven away because you didn't have enough confidence in God to take what He had given you, without condemnation, without self-pity, without un-godly regret, those among you — hear it: You could have had the promise. It was yours. He told you so. And if He's brought you back to the edge, if He's brought you again to the border of your destiny, you can still have what He said you could have. Step on in.

And one more thing: Eat before you go.

A very practical provision was made for Israel here, between the wilderness and the waters of the Jordan.

"Prepare provisions (the Hebrew word is 'tseydah' or 'tsedah,' meaning food, meat) for yourselves, for within three days you will cross over this Jordan, to go in to possess the land which the Lord your God is giving you to possess" (Joshua 1:11).

Eat up! Strength is needed — physical strength. We underestimate the importance of a good physical condition in matters related to God's Kingdom. Hear this carefully: We must be in the very best physical condition we can be in, given all relevant circumstances, all the while avoiding worship of the body and obsession with physical appearance. Our bodies are the human vessels through which God's life is released into the earth. Each of us has only one and it is finite. Because we are stewards of all that God has given us, we are stewards of our physical bodies. It is required of a steward that he be found faithful.

Several years ago I was happily engaged in asking God for increased anointing and new anointing and new levels of anointing when God stopped me cold and said, "You don't have the physical stamina necessary to sustain the levels of anointing and the kinds of anointing I want to give."

I remembered the story of a lady named Aimee Semple McPherson, an evangelist active in the early part of the 20th century, a lady with a miracle ministry and founder of the Foursquare Church. Now, I know that Aimee Semple McPherson had all kinds of problems and left all kinds of questions unresolved in regard to her ministry and her personal life. Nevertheless, Aimee Semple McPherson had a physical stamina that sustained a wondrous capacity for anointing. The lady stood and prayed in crowds of sick people and released to them healing from God for as long as 14 hours at a time. That requires physical energy and stamina that most of us don't have. We cry out for that kind of anointing; we lack the physical stamina to sustain it.

Our lack of physical energy and stamina has to do with stewardship of our appetites and our failure to properly steward our appetites for food, for rest and for exercise. It has to do with our lack of understanding regarding the appropriate value to be assigned the physical body as the vessel which carries the anointing of the Lord.

This disappointed people, Israel, was about to collide with the promise of her God and with new enemies of the promise. Physical strength was needed. Get food ready, Joshua told them. Eat! You're going to be carrying a lot of God around with you.

No Magic Here

We have identified a number of ingredients essential to this pre-curative tonic mixed for God's people and designed to ready them for God's promise. Of these ingredients, only five were administered at the very edge of that promise. These five included bone-jarring words from God that jolted the people out of a stuck-on-hold place; reiteration of the original charge a fresh charge — "in three days"; a new look at the land; and food to make them physically strong.

Those who are "into" numeric symbolism in the Bible, will want to note that five generally is identified as the number of grace. It may be interesting to consider whether these five are given as particular and specific measures of God's grace toward hearts rubbed raw in a long period of delay.

Other essential ingredients identified are qualities, positions and confidences that are laid into people over a long period of time, in relationship with God and in relationship with our companions in the Lord. These qualities would include confidence that God is up close and on our side and assurance that the march into the promise will be successful. (This calls for experiential knowledge of God and His Word, both written and spoken directly to our hearts.)

These qualities include, as well, separation to the words of

God's mouth; radical obedience; awareness of the consequences of disobedience; radical focus; strength and courage; a strong leader; for followers — confidence in the leader; and for leaders — confidence that followers will follow.

None of the "ingredients" — not even those that came in the hours preceding entrance into the promised land — none of them came by magic. God can work as quickly as He chooses — but He doesn't plop a disappointed people down at the edge of a promise, do a little sleight of hand, mumble some wonder-working words over our souls and then say, "There it is! Go for it!" He knows our frame; we are dust (Psalm 103:14).

Of course, it is truth; it's every bit truth: Hope deferred makes the heart sick; but when the desire comes it is a tree of life. There is no question here about the life-giving power of God-desire fulfilled in us. The question is: When the desire comes, will there be strength enough in human hands to seize, strength enough in the body, in the heart, in the spirit to possess, and will there be enough stick-to-it-ive-ness to hold on to the promise once it's possessed?

The tonic is for our humanity, to "plump up" rumpled bodies; to strengthen and tone-up and invigorate and activate tired systems; to remove the debilitating effects of hope-sickness in the hearts of people, or in the heart of a family or a church or a city or a nation.

God can work as quickly as He chooses, but God doesn't do magic. He wants His people engaged with Him in the process of dominion in the earth. He wants them hearing His words, responding, obeying, moving, acting with Him, laboring together with Him.

The wilderness of delay is not a place of just marking time until the Lord gets around to magic. It's a place for building, for laying in, for taking hold of God, so that the return to the edge of fulfillment is not just "same song, one more verse."

The wilderness is a place where things die. The wilderness is a place where things are born. At the first approach to the promise, there was stuff — circumstances, attitudes, fear, unbelief — that turned us away from God — yes, away from God. Those things fall dead in the wilderness. The things that have a capacity to carry us into the land come into life in the wilderness.

And…oh, yes, there's one more thing that has to happen on the way to the fulfillment of desire.

Chapter 10

In the Land

"When all the people were clean passed over,
…the ark of the Lord passed over, and the priests,
in the presence of the people…
When the priests that bare the ark of the covenant of the Lord
were come up out of the midst of Jordan…
The waters of Jordan returned unto their place
And flowed over all his banks, as they did before….
And the people came up out of Jordan on the tenth day of
the first month,
And encamped in Gilgal in the east border of Jericho."
Joshua 4:11, 18-19

In the land. That has a nice sound, doesn't it? The wilderness behind us…the Jordan behind us…

In the land…deferment becomes realization. What has been vision — a sense of distant possibility, always something away off out there, somewhere — now it's close. Now, if you wanted to, you could kneel down and dig your fingers into the soil. It's yours. God has given it to you. Begin to possess it. Begin to fill it with the purposes of God. Begin to do the wars of possession.

But first…a bit of business to address.

For the children of Israel it's been a long walk, and the final steps into the Jordan would not have been the easiest part. After all, only two among them would have had vivid, personal memory of walking on dry land through the midst of the Red Sea. For the others, at least for the first ones in line, stepping into the river must have been a bit scary, but once the waters rolled back and the dry ground appeared under their feet...Wow! This kind of God...One who rolls back rivers and seas...This God is the God Who has brought them to this place. This must be remembered.

God thought so, too.

"Those twelve stones that you put in the middle of the river, Joshua, and which you carried out of the river when everyone had passed through, pitch those stones in Gilgal. Set them up where you spend the night, one stone for each tribe."

The stones, of Joshua Chapter Four, were to be a memorial. In time to come there would be children and then grandchildren and then great-grandchildren who would see the stones and ask, "What do these stones mean?"

"When they ask," God said, "tell them you crossed the riverbed on dry land. Tell them I dried up the waters right in front of you, until all of you had crossed over, just as I did at the Red Sea. When it is remembered in the ears of all the people of the earth, then all the people of the earth will know that My hand is mighty, and they'll remember to fear Me forever."

Let's talk about stones.

There was a man of God named Sam Sasser. Once, I heard him speak of stones. He said stones are like hard places in our histories. Tough places. Painful places. They happened and they won't go away.

Sam Sasser said there are several things we can do with these hard places in our histories. We can put them in our pockets so every once in a while we can reach in and feel them and remind ourselves how hard our histories have been, how tough, how painful. Or we can line them up over our fireplaces and look at them every day and remember how hard this all has been, and we can show them to people who come to visit. We can talk about them. We can talk about the cuts on our feet that came when we walked through the stones and how hard it has been to carry the stones all this way and how hard it was to lift them up and put them up there above the fireplace. Or, Sam Sasser said, we can build an altar with them, and meet God there at that altar and remember Him.

It's important what we remember. God didn't tell Israel to remember the long walk or the death along the way or the disobedience or the out-and-out rebellion or the delay or the disappointment. God said to remember this: "Remember how I went ahead of you and cut off the waters of the Jordan before the ark of My covenant. Remember that I did it all for the sake of My presence among you."

And then God said, "Circumcise the sons of Israel again the second time."

All the grown men who had come out of Egypt, all the men of war, had died in the wilderness, along the way. The generation that would enter into promise had not been circumcised. We're not told exactly why they'd not been circumcised, although there's a bit of a clue in Joshua 5:6.

"…All the people who were men of war, who came out of Egypt, were consumed because they did not obey the voice of the Lord — to whom the Lord swore that He would not show them the land which the Lord had sworn to their fathers that He would give us, a land flowing with milk and honey."

Given this information, we can assume that the neglect of circumcision (verse 7) was another instance of failure to obey. No obedience; no milk and honey. And so Joshua circumcised the sons of those who'd died in the wilderness.

This corporate circumcision was more than just an exercise in mass surgical procedure. Apart from the covenant issues, circumcision is a means of guarding the procreative part of the male body from uncleanness that makes room for infection. We would do well, then, to make note of what happened here.

Back on the other side of the river, before Israel stepped into Canaan, God had jolted the nation to attention. He had given them a leader competent to lead the charge. He had reiterated the promise and made it fresh. He had shown Himself to be an up-close-and-personal God. He had instilled in them confidence that He would go with them and give them victory. God had given them everything necessary to get them on their feet and moving with a spring in their step.

Still, if you will hear this, in the place of procreation there had to be a cutting away of the flesh, which if not cut away would be a breeding ground for infection. Before the wars of possession could begin, flesh had to be cut away from what had been born and/or come to maturity in the wilderness. What had been born and/or come to maturity in that wilderness was a generation of people who would take hold of the promise of God and begin to possess it. But in such a generation, fresh up from the wilderness, there will be, nearly always, a residue of the pain of delay.

As I write these words I am in a place of circumcision. God has told me so. I have known the wilderness of delay. I have known the wilderness of disappointment. I have known the relentless sorrow of a heart that lives in promise unrealized. In those places the living Word of God has come to jolt me out of "stuck." He has given me all the things of which we spoke in chapters eight and nine, all the instruments and people and weapons, all the things necessary for possessing. He has given me tonic that has strengthened my muscles and bones, and I know what it is to be invigorated in the Spirit of God.

As well, I know what it is to have stepped into the land, with the remains of the long, long road hanging in deep folds from my heart, the residue of sorrow and disappointment and — less nobly — anger and resentment, memories of things God didn't tell me to remember. Some of those memories are hard and bitter. Some are just quietly painful. Sometimes only God sees the remains. Sometimes I see them. Sometimes others see them. In the remains of the wilderness are the places where infection can hide itself and grow and steal and kill and destroy.

The remains must be cut away. The heart needs a circumcision. What has been born and come to maturity in the wilderness is capable in God of possessing the land, but if the business of possessing is to be a clean and holy work — and it must be — then the remains of the wilderness must be cut away.

Isn't it odd that often we are reluctant to let go of all that flesh, as if somehow holding on to it...

Well...

Let the cutting come. Let the flesh fall away so that the things that we birth in the land will be born clean. After the circumcision...

"...They stayed in their places in the camp till they were healed" (Joshua 5:8).

Don't run off to fight the battles of possession hobbled by the pain of the surgery. Stand still. Wait until the bleeding stops. Wait until the goodness of God is more fresh in your mind and heart than the memory of the wilderness and its remains. I can't tell you how many seconds or hours or minutes or days or weeks or months it will be that you stand there, already in the land, waiting to be whole. You'll know. You'll know because the Captain of the Lord's Hosts will show up to say, "Take off your shoes. The ground you're standing on is holy" (Joshua 5:15).

When you hear these words, know that the wars of possession in the land of promise are about to begin.

A Final Note

This for the body of Christ:

A nurse told me this about circumcision: A proper circumcision is performed contemporarily by a rabbi, in a family setting, in a warm room with loving arms cradling the treasured child. The cut is quick and clean and over in an instant, and the child is comforted.

In many modern hospitals, however, the procedure is sterile in every sense of the word. There is a cold operating room, there is a child strapped to a cold surgical table, and the circumcision is a cauterization, a burning away of the flesh. It is a slower procedure without warmth and without comfort.

If we love God and walk with Him and seek after His purpose and His kingdom desires, then we have experienced or will experience or will experience again a season of deferred hope, with all the disappointment and sorrow of heart that accompanies such a season. Everyone who experiences such a season will stand in the land and know the cutting away of flesh from the things birthed in that season of delay.

This kind of circumcision, this circumcision of the heart, like the circumcision of the Old Testament, is evidence that covenant is in place. It speaks of the faithfulness of our God, Who has chosen us before the foundation of the world to be holy and without blame in His presence and Who is about the business of conforming us to the image of His dear Son.

The Church has been in some very long seasons of delay. There is a land just ahead of us. There are wars of possession to be accomplished. The feet of the battalions of God are bruised from the wilderness, but the feet will heal and the army will stand to the war.

It will be a mistake, however, for the house of God to ignore the fact that the army has a heart. When we set foot in the land, we will know circumcision of heart to a depth and to a degree of thoroughness we have not previously experienced in the house. We will experience it corporately. We will experience it individually.

We must awaken our spirits to see and hear. Wherever there is circumcision in progress, whether in a body of believers together or in an individual, in men and in women, wherever there are memories being cut away, wherever there is sorrow being cut away, wherever there is bitterness and anger and resentment being cut away, there is rawness and tenderness of heart that must be carried in careful arms and under the watchful regard of a warm house. This is our part to play, those of us who belong to the God of the covenant, the God of the Bible, your God and mine, ours.

Finally, it is to be remembered: Wherever there is circumcision in progress the God of hope is at hand. Lift up your heads! The King of glory, the Lord strong and mighty, the Lord mighty in battle (Psalm 24:8), the God Who does not lie (Numbers 23:19) has come your way. The promise is all around you. Take hold. Begin to possess.

ORDER FORM

"Healing Hope Deferred"

☐ YES, send me a copy of this book.

Name_____

Address_____

_____

City_____ State_____

Zip_____

Phone (optional)_____

Email (optional)_____

Amount Enclosed $_____

Book each: $12.95

Add $2.00 for shipping and handling.

(In Texas, add sales tax)

Mail order form to:
Sandra Martin
P.O. Box 227232
Dallas, TX 75222